THE HOME UNIVERSITY LIBRARY
OF MODERN KNOWLEDGE

CXVIII

THE BYZANTINE EMPIRE

THE
BYZANTINE EMPIRE

By

NORMAN H. BAYNES

OXFORD UNIVERSITY PRESS
LONDON   NEW YORK   TORONTO

First published in 1925, *and reprinted in* 1935, 1939 *and* 1944

CONTENTS

THE BYZANTINE EMPIRE

INTRODUCTION

An Empire to endure a death agony of a thousand years must possess considerable powers of recuperation. Until recently historians would have had us believe that the Byzantine state was perpetually in the article of death, although offering through the centuries a successful resistance to all assailants; but the colossal paradox only won credence through frequent repetition: it could not withstand the light of modern research. This little book is an attempt to sketch in brief outline some aspects of this East Roman civilisation, to recall the names of some of those famous men who were honoured in their generations and were the glory of their times.

But at the outset one question must be faced: from what period are we to recognise a distinctively Byzantine or East Roman Empire? For even when there was one ruler of the East in Constantinople and another in the West, in Milan or Ravenna, this did not impair the ideal unity of the Roman Empire: it was, in the words of a fourth-century writer, a " quasi-partition," of which the motive was administrative convenience. The same laws, the same principles of government, the same Roman traditions were acknowledged by both sovereigns. When in the year 476 Romulus Augustulus, the last Emperor of the West, ceased to reign, state theory remained unaltered; the " quasi-partition " having come to an end, the previous position was restored, and the rights of the western ruler passed automatically to the monarch in Constantinople—the joint authority was once more reunited in a single hand. Even with Justinian (527–565) it may be plausibly contended that the one characteristic which lends unity to his reign is his ambition to recover lost territory and to reassert the imperial prestige which had once belonged to his predecessors—that he is, in a word, the last of the Roman Emperors, and not yet a Byzantine.

Others again would choose as the decisive date that Christmas Day in Rome in the year A.D. 800 when, to his own surprise, Charlemagne was suddenly crowned by the Pope Emperor of the West. Henceforth there are indeed two Empires—the Holy Roman Empire of the West and the Byzantine Empire of the East. But however satisfying this view may be for the political theorist, or even for the historian of Western Europe, it is less useful for the student of the fortunes of East Rome. If the latter is to fix a moment for the beginning of his story, it must rather be the opening years of the seventh century, when the map of the Levantine lands assumed those features which were for ever after to determine the policy of Byzantine statesmen. Justinian's imperialism proved all too costly a vision for the Empire to realise : Mohammed had given unity to the Arab tribes through a common faith, and the warriors of the desert had burst with irresistible fury upon Palestine and Syria; their onrush had only been stayed by the mountains which guarded Asia Minor, while Africa was soon to fall into their hands; the Slavs had poured across the Danube, and in the Roman provinces was beginning that process of crystallisation into nationalities which ultimately formed the Balkan States of to-day. The first half of the seventh century is thus the distinctive period in which the historian would be inclined to place the rise of a " Byzantine Empire."

Yet this period, though in itself opening a new era compelling readjustments of policy and administration, is but the culmination of a long process, and can only be rightly understood in the light of the history of the three preceding centuries. For it is becoming increasingly clear that with the end of the third century of our era one link was closed, and mankind in the lands about the Mediterranean started to forge a new link in the chain of its history. That fresh beginning is marked by the recognition of Christianity by the state, and by the foundation of the city of Constantine—the New Rome set in the lands of the

Greek.   It is this event which must determine for us our point of departure.

In 1204 Constantinople was captured by the Crusaders, and Latin sovereigns took the place of the Byzantine monarchs. It is true that the old Roman Empire was restored in the course of the thirteenth century, but the Palæologi wear their crown with a difference : new influences from the West have interpenetrated the Roman world, and to New Rome herself there remains but the shadow of her former greatness. For this period much work remains yet to be done before the student can feel the ground secure beneath his feet : he attempts generalisations at his peril. For these and other reasons, in this little book the present writer has confined himself in the main to the period before the fall of Constantinople in the Fourth Crusade. Broadly, then, our survey extends from the founding of New Rome in the fourth century to its capture by the Crusaders in 1204.

CHAPTER I

THE CITY OF CONSTANTINE

"This city of the world's desire."—Constantine
the Rhodian : *Revue des Etudes grecques*, IX. (1896),
p. 38.

"In political institutions are the embodied
experiences of a race"; and never was this
truth more clearly manifest than in the work
of Diocletian and Constantine. The third
century had witnessed a widespread dis-
integration within the Roman world; both
military defence and social life seemed threatened with dissolution. Every frontier was
attacked; in Gaul, on the Rhine and on the
Danube barbarian hordes ravaged the provinces, while in the East the legions were faced
with the aggression of the Persian dynasty of
the Sassanids, who had risen to power (about
A.D. 212) on a tide of national enthusiasm.
Rome had lost her most capable rulers on the
field of battle, and her subjects in their own
defence elected generals and Emperors.
Patriotism had become local, because it could
no longer rely upon the protection of the
imperial armies. Society, menaced from without by overmastering forces, by the insolence
of the Army and by economic collapse from

within, must needs be clamped together by the imposition of rigorous fetters from which none might escape. Following in the footsteps of the Emperor Aurelian (A.D. 270–275), Diocletian forced the Roman citizen to carry on his father's trade or profession, and to sustain the liabilities of the guild of which his father had been a member; similarly under no circumstances was he permitted to free himself from his obligations to the state: were he landowner, were he town-councillor, were he frontier soldier, no matter what the personal sacrifice in liberty or property, he must stand at his post, and be haled back to his task if recalcitrant. In a hereditary caste system the stern genius of the Illyrian emperor saw the only hope for the ship of state, whose timbers were starting asunder.

The experiences of the third century further dictated the character of Diocletian's administrative reforms, for they had proved the need for effective generals, and for mobile armies; but those generals must be willing to remain subjects, and the armies must learn the lessons of obedience and discipline. From Rome's earliest days the provincial governor had been at once magistrate and, if the need arose, general: his single *imperium* conferred upon him an authority alike civil and military. But now the Empire's need demanded that an officer should be chosen solely for his military capacity, while little or no leisure remained for the discharge of his civil duties. Diocletian therefore completely separated the two careers, a measure for which the way had probably been prepared by the Emperor Gallienus (A.D. 253–268); he further excluded from the army the senatorial nobility, and appointed to military posts men of the middle classes (equites), who were recommended not by birth or wealth, but by capacity. At the same time he sought to meet the danger of an attempt on the part of a successful general to usurp the throne by increasing the number of the provinces and thereby reducing the forces under the command of any single officer. He organised the frontier defence, and probably took the first steps towards the creation of a mobile imperial army, a task subsequently carried to completion by Constantine (see ch. vii).

But it still remained to turn an unruly master into an obedient servant of the state. The authority of the Emperor must be re-established, and for this end Diocletian borrowed from the Sassanid court Persian conceptions of absolute sovereignty. The majesty of the purple should be hedged about with Oriental splendour and seclusion. The "Princeps" of the Early Empire, mixing freely with his fellow-citizens, should become the divine ruler withdrawn, remote, before whom his subjects must bow in abject prostration. The Emperor no longer founded his title to the throne upon the tumultuous acclamations of turbulent prætorians. His authority was derived from a divine delegation : his *imperium* was the gift of Heaven.

Thus Rome acknowledged her debt to the East. But this is no isolated instance : the life and thought of the Roman world had suffered a great change in the third century. Augustus after his victory at Actium (31 B.C.) had determined to base his power upon the western provinces, and under the Julio-Claudian house Gaul and Spain enthusiastically absorbed Latin culture. But the Hellenistic East continued to make its influence felt : in Juvenal's day the satirist could complain that the Syrian Orontes had flowed into the Tiber; in the third century, however, a current from the further East penetrated the Roman Empire, and the thought and culture of Persia seemed to be advancing to the conquest of the Levantine lands. Oriental cults were carried even into the western provinces, and the bowmen auxiliaries of the Roman army, continually recruited from Asia, bore with them to the camps on the Danube and the Rhine the worship of Mithras. The religious struggle of the third century appears as a contest between Eastern faiths; Latin paganism was fighting a losing battle : even the supporters of the old Pantheon—the Neo-Platonists—were employing the weapons furnished by the East; their mysticism was impregnated with Oriental elements, while their leaders were to be found in Egypt and Syria. The religious centre of the world had moved eastwards.

Literature too had deserted the Tiber, and Latin writers were outshone by their Greek rivals. Literary genius in the West finds its home in Gaul or Africa, not in Italy.

Further, it was on the Eastern and Northern frontiers that the barbarian peril was greatest. Claudius (A.D. 268–270) died while fighting against the Goths, and Valerian (A.D. 253–260) ended his life as a captive of Persia. Rome was too far distant alike from the Danube and the Euphrates.

The early Roman community was formed by farmers, not by seamen. Foreign trade could never naturally flow to Rome; the Tiber with its narrow channel and frequent floods was eminently unsatisfactory as a highway for sea-borne commerce. The capital of Italy had waxed rich on the spoils of the world, as, one by one, the vanquished kingdoms of the East had yielded their treasures to the conqueror. But when the Mediterranean had become a Roman sea, the tide of wealth turned. Italian agriculture declined, and the ruling classes abandoned the simplicity of their forefathers. The East supplied them with luxuries, and Italy did not produce that wherewith to pay for her imports. Each year a deficit had to be made good in specie; Italy became an impoverished land. The remorseless logic of economic laws likewise pointed to the East.

In a word, the religious, the literary, the military and the economic centre of the Empire had been displaced. A ruler wearing the diadem of a King of Kings called for an Eastern capital : here as elsewhere, it was left for

Constantine to complete the work of Diocletian, and to fix on a worthy site for the New Rome of the future. Thus on the peninsula which runs out from Europe to meet Asia, set in the midst between the Northern and the Eastern frontiers, protected from naval assault by the rapid tides of the Propontis, but yet possessing the magnificent harbour of the Golden Horn, there was built the city which was to stand through the centuries as the capital of the Empire, and the bulwark of the West.

Byzantium was re-christened after Constantine's final defeat of Licinius : the wall of the new city was begun at the same time as Constantius was made Cæsar : Nov. 8, 324. The rebuilding was hastened in 328, and on May 11, 330 was celebrated the solemn inauguration of Constantinople, and the Emperor with his court, his council (consistorium), his guard and his central administration took up his residence in the capital that bore his name.

Constantine had indeed yet another reason for this transference. Constantinople was to stand as a Christian city, while the capital on the Tiber long remained the stronghold of the older faith. The conversion of Constantine and the character of his own personal religious convictions have been the subject of unending controversy. But the brilliant work of the French scholar Jules Maurice on the numismatics of the period have demonstrated in the judgment of the present writer that without doubt Constantine had for himself definitely adopted Christianity as his creed, and that tradition is right in dating his conversion from his capture of Rome in October 312. The real glory of Constantine lies in this, that in an age which had no understanding for toleration he remained in general throughout his reign loyal to the policy upon which he and Licinius had agreed at their meeting in Milan in the month of February 313. The " Edict of Milan " may be a fiction, but it can hardly any longer be doubted that letters were sent from the imperial chancery to the governors of provinces directing them to permit all sects alike openly to profess their religious belief and to celebrate their own distinctive religious rites. Constantine in later years might act as an imperial missionary, might dissuade worshippers from attending pagan ceremonies, might attempt even to convert the Persian King of Kings, but he would not play the persecutor; he refused to " compel them to come in."

In his own newly-founded capital, however, he felt that it was open to him to make an exception from the principles adopted at Milan. After the solemn inauguration of A.D. 330 there should be no pagan rites celebrated in Constantinople. How then are we to explain the fact that at this time pagan temples were built, or at least rebuilt in the city? Maurice has suggested that these were erected between the years 324 and 330, and are the expression of the beliefs of officials who were themselves doubtless pagan; for the Christians had been swept from the civil service at the time of the so-called persecution of Diocletian. In these early years, it must be remembered, the Emperor was forced to effect his policy through a bureaucracy which was hostile to his aims, and even an Emperor's will can often enough make but slow progress against the solid weight of bureaucratic tradition. But in 330 Christian Constantinople was superimposed upon pagan Byzantium.

In the provinces the worship of the Emperor continued in a modified form; it was now merely a festival accompanied by no pagan sacrifices. In Umbria a temple was raised in honour of the Gens Flavia. Even in Constantinople itself a similar concession to the older faith must be attributed directly to the action of Constantine. Here on a lofty pillar there was raised a statue, which may have originally represented Apollo, but now bore the features of Constantine, while about the Emperor's head was set the rayed crown of Helios—the sun-god; this statue was revered by Christians and pagans alike. What is the meaning of this? Constantine claimed through Constantius Chlorus to be descended from the heroic emperor Claudius Gothicus, and it seems that Claudius, Constantius, and Constantine himself in his earlier days had all worshipped the solar deity, Sol Invictus—the Unconquered Sun. It has been suggested that Constantine desired through this statue to declare to his subjects that even after his conversion he still acknowledged his great ancestors; the new Flavian dynasty which he sought to found sprang from a glorious past, and could command the allegiance of all Romans. If this were indeed his aim, his desire was fulfilled; for on his death there is widespread evidence for the loyalty inspired by this dynastic sentiment.

One other concession Constantine made in the continued recognition of the Fortune (Tyché)—the tutelary spirit—alike of the old Byzantium and of Rome, though it may well be doubted whether the Emperor himself really directed, as Malalas asserts, that on the anniversary of the inauguration of the city his own statue bearing the Tyché should be carried in solemn procession through the hippodrome and reverenced by the reigning sovereign: all time-honoured usages were indeed habitually referred to Constantine. Modern scholars have perhaps attached too much importance to these idealised representations—the spirit of Byzantium with the ship's prow: for had she not the harbour which old Rome had lacked?—the spirit of Rome, whom Constantine would bring to dwell in the new Rome which he had founded for her. One is inclined to wonder whether the numismatist of some future age might not in like manner argue from the coins of the long fallen British Empire that in the twentieth century, beside the Christian Trinity, the worship of the goddess Britannia still persisted as a vestige of the ancient heathenism of the island.

But from one point of view there is no doubt
that the figure of the Tyché of Rome does serve
to recall for us Constantine's conception of his
city. The inhabitants of Constantinople are
the Populus Romanus, as appears from the
coins minted in the new capital; they are
granted the same privileges, they enjoy
(since 332) the same public distribution of
bread and wine and oil, for the grain-ships of
Egypt now sail to the Golden Horn, while the
same circus parties still continue the rivalries
of the Roman hippodrome. Constantine's
city was indeed New Rome. Her institutions
are modelled on the pattern of those of ancient
Rome, and Constantius II will raise the senate
of Constantinople to an equality with that of
the city on the Tiber. Constantine sought
by every means to encourage folk to leave
their homes, and to settle in his capital; the
Roman world was ransacked for art treasures :
Constantinople became a veritable museum
full of Greek and Hellenistic masterpieces,
while baths and churches, halls and squares
were planned on a scale of lavish magnificence.

This is no place for a topographical descrip-
tion of Constantinople—of its palace, that vast
complex of buildings to which successive
Emperors added during the centuries : of
its main street (the Mesé) running from S.
Sophia westwards through the Forum of
Constantine and the Forum Tauri to the
Golden Gate, the gate of triumphal entry :
of the porticoes, marble-faced, which lined the
Mesé, where were set the stalls of the hucksters :

of the narrow side streets, often only ten feet wide, rendered narrower still by the overhanging houses and external stairways : of the churches of the Holy Wisdom, of the Twelve Apostles, of S. Irene : of the circle of the walls enlarged by Theodosius II in the fifth century, and again by Heraclius in the seventh : for an account of all these the reader will turn to other books.

Enough if we realise at the outset how Constantine read the signs of the times, and what was his conception for his city. The pagan state had tried to exterminate the Christian Church and failed : Constantine endeavoured to lead the pagan state to enter into partnership with the Christian Church and succeeded : the city of Constantinople is the symbol of that union of Roman and Christian traditions, a union which only grew the closer through the years, until orthodox belief and Roman citizenship became synonymous.

CHAPTER II

SOCIAL LIFE IN THE EASTERN EMPIRE

" I observe, wherever I turn, that you are a most religious people."—Acts xvii. 2 (Moffatt's translation).

THE social life of the Eastern Empire awaits its historian.[1] In this brief chapter all that can be attempted is to suggest to the reader the general atmosphere of this Byzantine world, for until that is outlined further study is impossible.

It will hardly be denied that the interests and enthusiasms of our own age have been either scientific or social. Every question tends to become a social problem. In the East Roman Empire the interests and enthusiasms were religious : and questions whether social or political took a religious form. The Byzantine lived in a world where the supernatural was omnipresent and all-powerful. His holidays were religious festivals, his performances in his circus began with the singing of hymns, his trade contracts were marked with the sign of the Cross, or contained an invocation of the

[1] The present writer has for some years been collecting material for a study of popular life and thought in the Eastern Empire.

Trinity, his oracles were given by hermits or through visions accorded by the holy dead, his protection lay in consecrated amulets, the most powerful remedy in his pharmacopœia was the dust which contained a drop of sweat from the body of a stylite saint; his wars were crusades, his emperor the vice-gerent of God, while every startling event in nature was for him a special omen sent for his warning or encouragement.

The result of this outlook is that science was suspect. Much could be written in confirmation of this fact, but one true anecdote alone may often be more effective than a treatise. Once upon a time in the fourth century of our era Constantinople was visited by the plague, and large numbers of the citizens were dying daily. A doctor in the capital found that the mortality was disproportionately great among the poor factory hands living in narrow underground dwellings, and he gave expression to his belief that this was due to the lack of pure fresh air in these basement rooms. Constantinople was shocked: " Blasphemy ! " men cried—" a man's death was determined by God, and the question of air was irrelevant, impertinent ! " The doctor, however, continued to visit the poverty-stricken sufferers; at length he too caught the infection and died. Orthodoxy triumphed: it was Heaven's judgment upon the blasphemer.

Indeed when the doctor failed it was to the saint that the Byzantine instinctively turned. For as sufferers had come to sleep in pagan temples to be cured of their diseases, so now the Christian came to the Church or the Martyr's shrine.   The god who had once cured his worshippers while they slept in the Sosthenium near Constantinople—his identity is uncertain—was replaced by the Archangel Michael, who did the same. The pair of Christian doctors, the brothers Cosmas and Damian, were forced to explain in a vision to a Greek who sought healing that they were not the pagan twins Castor and Polydeukes (Pollux), but servants of the true God; yet on the Greek's conversion he was cured through the saints' intervention.   Cyril of Alexandria only effectually abolished the cult of the demon Menuthis by the transference of the remains of two martyrs, Cyrus and John, to the village where the false God was worshipped.   Sceptics might question whether the masterful Patriarch had not called into existence the sainted dead to serve his own purposes, but as Cyril's champion explained, though there were no earlier records of Cyrus and John, there was the Patriarch's word for it : surely that ought to satisfy any reasonable seeker after truth—and certainly Cyrus and John, like Menuthis before them, brought healing to sufferers in their sleep.   But the most interesting illustration of the practice is to be found in the seventh-century miracles of Artemius (martyred in the fourth century), the sainted specialist for all diseases of the genital organs, whose delicacy forbade him to treat female patients directly, but who in their case acted through his assistant S. Febronia, a lady who had, like himself, departed this life some centuries before. These contemporary accounts, however, though full of a rich unconscious humour, hardly admit of reproduction here. From all parts of the Empire diseased folk travelled to Constantinople, and the general practice according to these Miracula was for the patient to come to the Church of S. John the Baptist, in which was the shrine of S. Artemius, on Saturday evening : he would spread his mattress on the floor as near the shrine as possible, and the saint, if inclined to heal the sufferer, did so while the latter slept, generally at the same time appearing in a vision to the sleeper. But Artemius was by no means bound by considerations of locality : he could even heal a worshipper on the high seas.

In a similar way the Christian saint tends to take the place of the pagan patron god of the city. Such is the position of S. Demetrius at Thessalonica, while the capital always enjoyed the special protection of the Virgin Mother of God. As S. Demetrius appeared at the head of the East Roman troops in the defence of his city, so when besieging Constantinople the Chagan of the Avars saw a majestic female form pacing along the battlements and leading the Romans as they left the city gate. That vision of Demetrius, the horseman of God, as it is painted for us in the Miracula S. Demetrii, carries us backward to the intervention of the Dioscuri at Lake

Regillus, carries us forward to the battlefields of France in 1914, when S. George, we are told, appeared at the head of the English troops, and turned to flight their foes.

This continual consciousness of the presence of the supernatural forms the frame in which the life of the Byzantine citizen is set. In great things or in small his passion for theology remains; the unseen world is with him late and soon. The Army revolting demanded of the Emperor Constantine IV that he should take as his colleagues his brothers Heraclius and Tiberius : why? "We believe in the Trinity," they proclaimed, "let us then crown three Emperors." Even when a large dog sprang out on Bishop Parthenius of Lampsacus "it came, I take it," says his biographer, "not from any house, but from the Unseen Dog " —the Devil. Fortunately the Bishop had sufficient presence of mind to make the sign of the Cross and so escaped unharmed. A trifling incident, no doubt, but it serves to illustrate the outlook of the East Roman.

The inhabitant of the capital lived not only in a religious atmosphere but also in an atmosphere of danger : in some centuries his nerves must have been continually on the strain, for his city underwent siege after siege, and in this constant tension we may find an explanation of some of the less admirable traits of the Byzantine character. It may at least be argued that the Roman Empire in the West fell simply through the fact that it was outnumbered : had some inventive brain produced gunpowder and a gun, the invasions could have been repelled, for this would have been sufficient to counteract the numerical deficiency of the Romans. In some sense the walls of Constantinople represented for the East the gun and gunpowder, for lack of which the Empire in the West perished. But even walls must be manned, and if the defenders are too few, subtlety, diplomacy, fraud undisguised, if need be, must play their part; and thus was intensified that tendency towards an unprincipled acuteness, which may be traced in the characters even of the Greeks of the days of Pericles and Demosthenes. Self-interest unscrupulously gratified is, it must be freely admitted, all too common among East Romans, both of high and low degree.

And constant strain by reaction produces excess. That among Byzantine characteristics violence, brutality and cruelty do play a part it would be idle to deny. That part has of course been grossly exaggerated, but it cannot be ignored. In its vengeance on unpopular statesmen, in the facility with which arson and murder became the frequent accompaniments of any riot, the populace of the capital was capable of a reckless disregard for human life, while by a system of punishment which relied mainly on mutilation—the cutting off of the hand, the slitting of the nose, the blinding of the eyes—the government failed in its turn to set a good example.

It has been suggested that this cruelty may

have been aggravated by the fact that savage races became incorporated from time to time in the body politic, only veiling their barbaric origin by a thin cloak of Hellenism; but for this frame of mind may not the instant peril to which Constantinople was continually exposed have been in part responsible? The present writer is no psychologist, but he would suggest that the city's power of self-control may have been weakened by the very violence of the nervous tension in which it was kept. Often enough, if you ventured beyond the gates of the capital to indulge a passion for hunting, a favourite pastime of the Byzantines, you could not have known whether you would return—at the beginning of the eighth century, we are told, only those who had provisions to last *three* years might remain within the walls, so great was the danger. We do not always realise the price which the inhabitants of Constantinople paid for their defence of Europe.

But despite the peril the East Roman demanded that he should be amused. The three centres of the life of Constantinople were the Palace, the race-course and the Cathedral. "If S. Sophia," Rambaud once said, "belonged to God, and the Palace to the Emperor, the hippodrome was the possession of the people." If the baths were shut and the hippodrome closed, life for the Byzantine had lost its savour and become stale, flat and unprofitable.

Built by Septimius Severus (A.D. 193–211),

the hippodrome existed before Constantinople was born, and it stands to-day, though the Palace of the Emperor has vanished. The Circus parties of the Blues and Greens were organised as a city militia : their corporations, representing the populace of Byzantium, stand as autocracy's concession to the old ideal of the city state. The political battles of former centuries were stilled, but the ruthless passion for the interests of a party was only transferred to another sphere, and the mere fact that Blues and Greens now sat opposite each other on different sides of the hippodrome and in concert hurled their envenomed taunts across the race-course only lent a new cohesion and solidarity to their unions. The question has often been raised why the early Emperors of Constantinople permitted the turbulence of the Circus parties : an obvious answer is that even the power of an autocrat is bounded by limits which he did not set, but it is also true that the monarch might see in the mutual antagonisms of the Blues and Greens a safety valve by which a way of escape was opened for evil humours which might otherwise have threatened his own throne.

Think for an instant of what this many-sided hippodrome meant for the Byzantine world. Consider the army of folk it employed —guards, trainers, stablemen, charioteers : think of the host of performers, male and female; for between the morning and after-noon chariot races there were exhibitions given by pantomimists and acrobats, by rope-walkers who dressed and undressed on the tight-rope, and by those who balanced a pole on their foreheads up which boys climbed and postured at its top. In the early days of Constantinople too there were fights with wild beasts in the Circus so that a staff of keepers was a necessity; Acacius, the father of the Empress Theodora, was a bear-warden, and she herself a pantomime actress. The charioteers lived in a world where pagan superstitions still flourished; by magic charms and amulets they sought to bind their competitors beneath a spell and compass their defeat. Before the races the drivers were searched to see that they did not carry some magical mascot which might unfairly secure them the victory. Thus curses upon the heads of hated rivals were frequently written on small lead tablets, of which we still possess large numbers. Here figure traces of a debased Gnosticism, appeals to Egyptian gods—Osiris, Seth, Typhon—to the holy angels and archangels, to the Powers of the lower world and to an enigmatical Being, the holy Eulamon. From these tablets we can learn the names of the horses : generally stallions—among them Phœbus, Achilles, Babylonios, Audax—while fragments of the technical sporting vocabulary of the fourth and fifth centuries can be recovered. These tablets, it is true, come from Rome, but here the new capital had merely taken over an institution from the old, and we may safely conclude that the conditions of circus life in the East were closely similar to those of the West.

Every reader will picture the scene for himself : the serried ranks of Greens and Blues in their thousands, the patricians and senators in their gorgeous robes of silk and flashing jewels seated on the terrace reserved for them : high above the course, connected with the palace and cut off from the Circus itself, the boxes of Empress and Emperor. The long suspense : then the arrival of the imperial guard : a movement : the Emperor enters his box : he raises his mantle, and makes the sign of the Cross. The choirs sing, and strangely mingled with praises to the Christ and the Virgin pour the passionate supplications for the victory of this or that charioteer. Then the cars burst away : Triumph ! Defeat !—and later under cover of night in the dark passage-way of the narrow street a knife gleams for an instant, and a body falls : a splash in the sea and the current sweeps something away. A " Green " has had his revenge on a victorious " Blue.'

But the hippodrome is more than a race-course : it is an assembly—a substitute for the vanished Comitia, the last asylum of the liberties of the Populus Romanus. Here the people forgetting the rivalry of the " colours " can call an Emperor to account, or demand the dismissal of a hated minister. Anastasius, accused of heterodoxy, will appear here uncrowned and will profess to his subjects his readiness to abdicate. Here, too, Belisarius will stifle the " Nika " Rebellion in a bath of blood.

Our great essayist with masterly brevity summarised the causes and motives of seditions as " innovation in religion, taxes, alteration of laws and customs, breaking of privileges, general oppression, advancement of unworthy persons, strangers, dearths, disbanded soldiers, factions grown desperate; and whatsoever in offending people joineth and knitteth them in a common cause " (Bacon, *Of Seditions and Troubles*). The history of the hippodrome of Constantinople could provide an illuminating commentary upon this text.

The race-course is also the scene of imperial triumphs where emperors place the purple boot—the symbol of sovereignty—upon the heads of defeated rivals or conquered foes. It is a court of criminal justice, where judges regularly sit : here even an Emperor convinced of the crime of a minister may order the offender, as did Theophilus, to be burned alive before his subjects' eyes. A popular Emperor was Theophilus ! The Circus too saw those processions where a disgraced courtier or priest was exposed to the mockery of the crowd, often seated on an ass, but facing its tail. It was a Museum where the treasures of ancient sculpture were collected, where the official hierarchy of the Christian Church, having come to terms with the Circus which it had so furiously abused, gazed upon the pagan gods whom Christianity had displaced. The hippodrome is a mirror of the Byzantine world.

The citizen of the East Roman Empire had in fact two heroes—the winner in the chariot race and the ascetic saint. In honour of the former he raised pictures and statues everywhere: to the charioteer were given special privileges, for example, he was freed from any liability to corporal punishment, while to him the *littérateurs* addressed their choicest epigrams. But to the ascetic came the pilgrims from every side, led by a passionate longing to see the saint on his pillar, to gain his benediction, to carry off one of those little images of the holy man which were manufactured wholesale for the needs of the pious; and this image with a lamp burning before it would protect the pilgrim's shop and home from harm, would give him a new confidence and a fresh sense of security amidst the perils of his life.

And if we may follow our pilgrim to his home we shall find there a strong feeling for the unity of the family, and great mutual devotion. Woman is mistress of the household, and was able to exercise in her own sphere a remarkable influence over her husband and her children; how powerful that influence was we may learn from the portrait which Psellos has drawn for us of the mother whom he revered (cf. Diehl, *Figures byzantines*, Ser. I, ch. xi).

The daughter was married at an early age: the choice of a bridegroom was a matter of family arrangement, and the bride had rarely, it appears, seen her husband before

B

marriage. Yet, though respectable women would not visit the theatre, the Byzantine wife was by no means a prisoner in her home, and her seclusion has sometimes been exaggerated. The East Roman theory of sovereignty knew nothing of morganatic marriages, and the imperial stock was often strengthened by the choice of a bride taken from the middle classes : occasionally the Emperor would even select his partner from a bevy of the fairest damsels drawn from the provinces for the purpose.

The historian of the social life of the later Empire will indeed draw his material from many sources : he will illustrate its irresponsible humour from the pumpkin effigy of the Chazar chieftain which cost the inhabitants of Tiflis their lives, its heroic endurance from the defence of the frontier towns against Persia, its simple piety from the lives of Stylite saints, while the religious chronicle will be enlivened by the antics of those who became "Fools for Christ's sake." The Farmer's law and monastic records will enable him to sketch, at least in outline, the life of the village; the Book of the Prefect will give a new vividness to his picture of the trade life of the capital—of the fishermen reporting their daily catch to the city authorities, of the sellers of linen goods carrying their wares on their shoulders, and of the peasants driving in their swine to market. From the biography of Theodore the Syceote he will sketch the country schoolboy, the life of John the

Almsgiver will make seventh-century Alexandria more real to him, seventh-century Thessalonica will be illustrated by the miracles of S. Demetrius, and seventh-century Constantinople by those of S. Artemius. From the Epic of Digenis Akritas he will picture the border forays waged between Christian noble and Saracen emir, while Kekaumenos in his ripe old age will, like another Polonius, sum up for him the worldly wisdom of East Rome in the eleventh century.

Meanwhile let the reader run through the Chronicle of Malalas and from that strangely mixed record of public affairs as viewed from Antioch he may obtain some conception of the things which really interested the good citizens of the Eastern Empire : with a little imagination he will at once supply the missing headlines and his own Sunday paper will appear as a flagrant plagiarism; thus apart from war news—intelligence from the Eastern front is naturally given in most detail—he may note such items as " Prisoners of War Relief Fund opened. Generous response to the appeal " (*Mal.*, p. 461, Bonn ed.). " Wonderful Display of Shooting Stars. What does it portend ? " (p. 477). " Italian's marvellous performing dog " (p. 453). " Horrible scandal in the Church. Shocking charges against well-known Bishops " (p. 436). " An audience with an Abyssinian King. Weird Etiquette of an Oriental Court " (p. 457). " The White Slave Traffic in Constantinople. Royalty intervenes " (p. 440). " Sunday observance :

a new law passed " (p. 371). " The Law's
delays : Exemplary punishment of corrupt
Barristers " (p. 384). " Fire in a Theatre.
Lighted candles cause conflagration. Flames
rapidly extinguished " (p. 467). " New Baths
opened : Ingenious heating installation "
(p. 359). " Expulsion of Ballet-dancers.
Special favour shown to Alexandria's Corps
de Ballet " (p. 417). " Earthquakes in
Antioch. Terrible damage and loss of life "
(often recurs). " The Jewish Massacres : The
Emperor's witty remark " (p. 389). The list
could be prolonged indefinitely.

Of the great ones of the Byzantine world,
of the pomps and splendours of its court, we
can learn from any history of the Empire :
we need rather to recover the life of the middle
classes, the outlook of the ordinary citizen.
For their reconstruction the writers of the
past have drawn from the sermons of
Chrysostom, a moralist painting the sins of
his day : they have gone to the Secret History
of Procopius—a work written in an hour of
embitterment and despondency : and from
sources such as these they have pictured a
society corrupt, vicious, luxurious and degener-
ate, a theatre entirely given over to obscenity,
to the revue and the pantomime, a world
where monks lived with nuns in ambiguous
sanctity, where courtesans spurred sated lust
by wearing the robes of virgins dedicated to
God. But the story of the pander and the
prostitute is an incomplete chronicle of any
great civilisation : the record of East Rome

is something far richer, far more many-sided. It may be doubted whether any Empire can live by vice alone: it is certain that the Byzantine Empire never made the attempt.

CHAPTER III

A LIST OF THE BYZANTINE EMPERORS

"What! will the line stretch out to the crack of doom?"—*Macbeth*, Act IV. sc. i.

NOT a few students on first viewing a table of the sovereigns of East Rome must have shared Macbeth's sentiment of horror. This little book cannot attempt to summarise the annals of the Byzantine Empire : but it may be convenient at the outset to remind the reader of the succession of the monarchs who governed from Constantinople. This chapter is thus essentially a chronological list to which a few comments have been added.

PERIOD I. A.D. 337–518

CONSTANTINIAN DYNASTY, 324–363.

    CONSTANTINE I dies 337 : the army demands to be governed only by the sons of the great Emperor : other relatives are massacred, but Julian is spared on account of his youth. The Empire is divided between

    CONSTANTIUS II, 337–361, and his brothers, Constantine, 337–340, and Constans I, 337–350 : Constantius becomes sole ruler in 350, but only overcomes the usurper Magnentius in 351 at the great battle of Mursa between Drave and Danube, where 54,000 Roman troops are said to have been slain. Julian

(cousin of Constantius), commanding in Gaul,
is hailed Emperor, 360, and succeeds on the
death of Constantius in 361.

JULIAN the Apostate, 361–363, is killed on the
retreat from Persia and the army hurriedly
elects

JOVIAN, 363–364. On his death civil and military
authorities deliberate, and elect as emperor a
soldier, Valentinian I (Feb. 364–375), who in
March makes his brother Valens his colleague,
and leaves the latter to govern the East.

VALENS, 364–378, fell fighting against the Goths at
the battle of Adrianople, 378, and Gratian (son
of Valentinian), ruling in the West appoints
as his colleague for the East the Spanish
General Theodosius.

THEODOSIAN DYNASTY, 379–457

THEODOSIUS I the Great, 379–395 (emperor of
East and West since 392); on his death his
son Honorius (395–423) rules in the West, and
in the East his son

ARCADIUS, 395–408, who is succeeded by his seven-
year-old son

THEODOSIUS II, 408–450. 408–414 administration of Anthemius prætorian præfect.

In 414 Pulcheria, sister of the Emperor,
becomes all powerful, then for a time (431–
441) Eudocia, the Athenian wife of Theodosius
II, was able to assert her authority. From 441
until a few months before the death of
Theodosius II the eunuch Chrysaphius was
master in Constantinople.

On the Emperor's death Pulcheria marries
Marcian the veteran soldier from Thrace and
thus confers on him the throne.

MARCIAN, 450–457. On his death no successor had
been appointed, but the all-powerful master
of the soldiers, the Alan Aspar, himself an
Arian and therefore excluded from the throne,
creates Leo, a military tribune from Dacia,
Emperor.

Leonine Dynasty, 457–518.

Leo I, 457–474, to free himself from Aspar and his
Gothic troops, turned to the Isaurians, and
married his daughter Ariadne to Tarasicodissa,
who assumes the name of Zeno (468).   Aspar
is murdered (471).   Leo is succeeded by
Ariadne's son

Leo II, 474, who makes his father Zeno his
colleague, and dies.

Zeno, 474–491.   On his death in 491 no successor
had been appointed, and, following the
precedent of 450, Ariadne nominates as
Emperor Anastasius of Dyrrachium, one of
the palace guards, recently selected as candidate for the see of Antioch.

Anastasius, 491–518, dies childless.

First Period.   337–518

In this period the reign of Theodosius I
marks a central point; he definitely founded
the Orthodox state and broke with the theory
of toleration for pagans, while in external
politics he concluded a peace with Persia
which ended for more than a century the
ceaseless war on the eastern frontier.   The
fourth century demonstrated the narrowness
of that margin which guaranteed the defence
of the empire's boundaries.   Constantius was
forced to call troops from Gaul to defend the
Asiatic provinces, and despite the success of
Julian the Apostate at the great battle of
Strassburg (357), despite the heroic efforts
of the frontier Emperor Valentinian, it became
clear that the German invasion could not be
permanently checked by the barrier of the
Rhine.   If the fourth century saw in the West

EEC.	664	500.
MEC.	560	886
LEC.	087	552.
MEC.	579	924
PER.	790	161.

26-80
62-5-
134-60

20.00
58-60.
100-00.

375.0.

502-50

the Romanisation of barbaric tribes, it also witnessed the beginning of the barbarisation of Roman culture. The terrible defeat of the Imperial forces by the Goths at Adrianople (378) appeared to foreshadow a similar Gothic triumph in the East : the peril was averted for the time by the heroism and statesmanship of Theodosius the Great. Throughout the fourth century Armenia had been the apple of discord between Persia and Rome, as was Afghanistan between Russia and England in the nineteenth. The sympathies of the Armenian nobility inclined towards Persia. Wiser than his modern critics, Theodosius realised that the continued existence of Armenia as an independent state was dearly purchased at the price of continuous frontier wars; he accordingly agreed to a treaty whereby the country was partitioned between the two Empires. When, at the death of Marcian, Aspar with his Goths and Alans threatened to play the part assumed by Ricimer in the West, Leo I could take the Isaurians into partnership and unhindered by peril from Persia could strike, and strike hard. The Isaurians saved the East from barbarian domination, and when their work was done they were expelled from the capital by Anastasius. " New Rome " the queen of cities had been christened, and Roman she remained.

But, when peace with Persia was secured, the Empire was still on the defensive, for the Finno-Ugrian Huns were devastating the

Danube lands : Cyrus, præfect of Constantinople under Theodosius II, completed the massive barrier of the landward fortifications : here was " a wall in very truth " as was declared by the inscription which commemorated the great achievement ; the work was well done ; not till the fourth crusade would the sovereigns of East Rome see their city in the hands of the enemy.

In the sphere of religion the short restoration of paganism under Julian the Apostate only served to show that the old faith was no longer a serious rival to Christianity. The danger was rather that the Church, which had given new life to the Empire, should itself be split in twain by theological differences. The triumph of orthodoxy, championed by Athanasius, was at length assured ; but Athanasius was patriarch of Alexandria, and from 381 to 451 the duel between Constantinople and Alexandria for ecclesiastical supremacy was fought out with increasing bitterness. At the council of Chalcedon (451) the struggle was decided in favour of Constantinople, but the definition of orthodox faith formulated by the Fathers only gave birth to fresh disputes.

When Christianity triumphed in Syria, it awoke a Syriac literature and something approaching a national consciousness, while the Egyptians had never ceased to form a nation. In a theological age nationalism found its expression in heresy—in the belief in the presence of but one nature in the incarnate Christ, in opposition to the two natures asserted by the Chalcedonian confession of faith. How could the Eastern Church conciliate Syrian and Egyptian nationalism, and still remain in communion with Rome? This was the problem which vexed the reigns of Zeno and Anastasius. They capitulated before the East, and broke off communion with the West (see ch. v).

PERIOD II. A.D. 518–610

JUSTINIANEAN DYNASTY, 518–602.

JUSTIN I, 518–527. The uneducated Illyrian, Justin, commander of the palace guard, being given gold by the eunuch Amantius to secure the throne for the latter's nephew, employs it to win over the troops in his own behalf, and is thus acclaimed Emperor. The government, however, really rested with his nephew,

JUSTINIAN I, 527–565, who is succeeded in turn by his nephew,

JUSTIN II, 565–578, who soon became insane; in a lucid interval Justin II created Tiberius, count of the palace guards, Cæsar (Dec. 574), and before his death crowned him Emperor.

TIBERIUS II, 578–582. In 582 Tiberius II betrothed his daughter to his general Maurice, and a day before his own death crowned Maurice Emperor.

MAURICE, 582–602, is overthrown and assassinated by the rude barbarian Phocas, the ringleader in a mutiny of the Danube army.

PHOCAS, 602–610.

SECOND PERIOD. 518–610

The outstanding feature of this period is Justinian's attempt to reclaim for Rome the lands now occupied by the barbarians, and to establish the will of the sovereign as the sole law within the recovered Empire. Africa was wrested from the Vandals, and Italy from the Goths, while in Spain a Roman province with its centre at Cordova heralded the realisation of Justinian's imperial dream. Within the capital the power of the Circus parties was broken, the Church acknowledged the lord of Constantinople as priest-king, and communion with Rome was restored. A new Church of the Holy Wisdom rose as sign and symbol of a splendour which outvied even Solomon's in all his glory. And yet Justinian's very success was disastrous, for it was undermined by irreconcilable contradictions. The Emperor was fired by a passionate desire to reform the administration, to lighten the burdens and the hardships of the provincials; but if taxation was to be lessened, the treasury must suffer, and alike for his reconquests, for the defence of the threatened frontiers and for his great building schemes money—and ever more money—was essential; Justinian was thus forced to tolerate the unscrupulous exactions of his hated minister of finance, John of Cappadocia. Again if the new conquests in Italy were to be secured, the Eastern Church was bound to be at peace with the Roman see; but the acknowledgement of Chalcedonian orthodoxy meant the disaffection of mono-physite Syria and Egypt. To save the restored unity of the West, the loyalty of the East was jeopardised. Further the Emperor, sprung from a Latin-speaking province, felt himself to be a missionary, proclaiming the old Roman idea of empire, codifying Roman law, encouraging its study, and upholding the use of the Latin tongue; meanwhile West and East were ever less and less capable of understanding one another, and the East in thought and sentiment was growing more and more Greek; it was precisely the Danube provinces which might have formed a link between the two worlds that were now being overrun by Slav and Bulgar. Lastly even Nature herself rose against Justinian: he needed a ready supply of soldiers for his armies, yet in 542 and the following years the Empire was scourged by a visitation of the plague which carried off those who should have fought the Empire's battles. The hunger for men crippled Justinian's military activities.

In a word, the resources of the Empire broke down before the task that Justinian demanded of them. Justin II sought to follow in his uncle's steps and his mind succumbed beneath the intolerable burden. Tiberius abandoned Justinian's policy: the Empire could not wage a struggle on two fronts: could not stem the flowing tide of Slav and Avar in the European provinces, and at the same time make head against the new aggression of the Persian monarchy. The heart of the Empire was in Asia, and Asia must be saved at all costs: thus Italy fell to the Lombards, and barbarians occupied the Danube lands. When happy chance had enabled

Maurice to make a favourable treaty with Persia (590), he turned once more to the defence of the Northern frontier, but the army refused to bear the hardships of the campaign, and Maurice lost throne and life. Under Phocas Persian invasions, barbarian devastation and domestic strife brought Romania to the very verge of destruction. A provincial revolt brought salvation to the Empire.

PERIOD III. A.D. 610–717

HERACLIAN DYNASTY.

Phocas was overthrown by an expedition from the province of Africa headed by
HERACLIUS, 610–641. On his death he left by his first marriage a son Constantine (III), and by his second marriage with his niece Martina (among other children) a son Heracleonas (crowned in 638). He is thus succeeded by

CONSTANTINE III, 641
and   } as joint Emperors, but the
HERACLEONAS 641

army refused to submit to the rule of Martina, and on the death from consumption of Constantine III, Heracleonas was forced to crown his nephew Constans, the grandson of Heraclius I, as Emperor (September 641), and towards the end of September in the same year he and his mother were overthrown, and

CONSTANS II, 641–668, became sole Emperor. Constans was murdered in Sicily and was succeeded by his son

CONSTANTINE IV, 668–685, who was followed by his sixteen-year-old son

JUSTINIAN II, 685–695. Rendered unpopular by his arbitrary and oppressive government, he was dethroned in 695 by his general in the East, Leontius, and banished to Cherson.

JUSTINIAN IN BANISHMENT.

LEONTIUS, 695–698, was overthrown when the
sailors of the fleet, revolting in Crete, declared
for their vice-admiral Apsimar, who became
Emperor as

TIBERIUS III, 698–705. But in 705 Justinian with
the help of the Bulgarian chieftain Terbel is
restored.

JUSTINIAN II, 705–711. Cherson, fearing Justinian's tyranny, revolts under an Armenian
officer, Philippicus Bardanes, and is joined by
the Chazars. The fleet sent against Cherson
makes common cause with the rebels. Justinian II is deserted by his army and killed.

DECLINE OF IMPERIAL POWER.

BARDANES, 711–713. His ill-success leads to the
elevation of the civilian secretary of state

ANASTASIUS II, 713–716, but his attempt to restore
discipline in the army induces the troops of the
theme or military province (cf. chapter viii) of
Opsikion to declare as Emperor the insignificant
provincial official

THEODOSIUS III, 716–717; but salvation came with
the accession of the general of the Anatolic
theme, Leo the Syrian, or, as he is commonly
known, the Isaurian.

THIRD PERIOD.   610–717

From Africa, where the Latin element was
now strongest, Heraclius sailed to rescue the
Roman Empire : the voyage was in his eyes
a religious undertaking, and throughout his
reign the religious interest was paramount.
In his war with the fire-worshippers, in which
he penetrated into the heart of Persia, he was
warmly supported by the Church. After
six years of ceaseless campaigning his victory

was complete, but his health was ruined. And at this moment the tribesmen of Arabia, driven forth by the increasing desiccation of the peninsula to seek more fertile lands, were for the first time in their history united by a common faith. The armies of the Mohammedans wrested Palestine and Syria from the Empire; a few years later Egypt was lost. It is an important moment in Byzantine history, for the territory which Rome retained was the land of orthodoxy : the strongholds of the Monophysites were lost. The Eastern Church had no further need to conciliate heretics : she became the Orthodox Church of the Orthodox Empire : for the future, church and state were indissolubly connected.

As was suggested in the Introduction, it is somewhere about the middle of the seventh century that the Levantine world assumed those peculiar features which were to characterise the course of Byzantine history. The Slavs, freed from their Avar task-masters, acknowledge the overlordship of the Empire, and overrun the Danube provinces, penetrating into Greece, and even making their way to the islands of the Ægean. The greater part of Italy is lost to the Lombards, and in the older capital the Pope is free to step into the room of the absent Emperors, for, though Constans might seek to make of Southern Italy and Sicily a strong outpost of the Empire against the advance of the Arabs in the West, his policy was not followed by his successors. The heart of the Empire is now in Asia—in

Greek-speaking lands : the enmity with Persia which Constantinople had inherited from the earlier Rome gives place to the hostility with Islam, which was to endure as long as the Empire stood. Distinctively Byzantine history has begun.

The glory of the Heraclian house lies in the fact that it met the first shocks of the Arab invasion and stayed it south of the Taurus range : when the enemy took to the sea the capital resisted all attacks. Every year from 673 to 677 Moawiyā sailed from his naval base at Cyzicus, and every year he retired discomfited, concluding a peace in 678. The province of Africa might fall to the Mohammedans (697), Isperich might found a Bulgarian kingdom between the Danube and the Balkans; but Constantinople stood as the protectress of Europe, and behind her walls civilisation was safe. In the confusion which followed the overthrow of the Heraclian house it looked as though the defence was giving way; but once more incapacity was swept aside, and a strong hand seized the helm of the threatened state.

PERIOD IV. A.D. 717–867

ISAURIAN DYNASTY (Iconoclasts), 717–802.

LEO III, 717–741, is succeeded by his son

CONSTANTINE V, 741–775, who is followed on the throne by his son

LEO IV, 775–780. On his death his widow Irene undertook the government for her young son

CONSTANTINE VI, 780–797. Although the troops compelled her to retire from the regency in

790, Constantine restored her to power in 791,
and in 797 she overthrew and blinded her own
son, and thus became Empress without a
colleague.

IRENE, 797–802, was overthrown by a conspiracy
of high officials in 802, and was succeeded by
the imperial treasurer, Nicephorus.

END OF ISAURIAN DYNASTY.

NICEPHORUS, 802–811, fell fighting against the Bulgarians. His son

STAURACIUS, 811, escaped, though badly wounded,
and created as Emperor his father-in-law

MICHAEL I, 811–813, whose defeat by the Bulgarians
was probably due to the treachery of the
Armenian general who overthrew him, and
ascended the throne as

LEO V, 813–820. Leo was murdered at the altar
in 820, and a rude provincial from Amorion
in Upper Phrygia, who was now commander
of the guard, became emperor.

PHRYGIAN DYNASTY, 820–867.

MICHAEL II, 820–829. He was followed by his
learned son

THEOPHILUS, 829–842, at whose death his widow
Theodora acted as regent for his young son

MICHAEL III, 842–867; Michael's favourite, Basil
the Macedonian, removed at the Emperor's
wish the all-powerful Cæsar Bardas, brother of
Theodora (866), and, himself created Cæsar in
the same year, then secured the Emperor's
murder.

FOURTH PERIOD. 717–867

In the first year of Leo's reign the Arabs
began their supreme attack upon Constantinople. Muslama encamped before the city
with the land army in August 717; the fleet
under Suleiman appeared in September.

Throughout the hardships of a winter of extraordinary severity the blockade continued, until at length in August 718 the baffled assailants were forced to abandon the siege. Never again was Europe in such deadly peril from the Arab : the great crisis had found the great man.

Church historians, however, could not forget that Leo was the first of the Image-Breakers (see ch. v) : monkish chroniclers never forgave him or his successors. But even they cannot obscure the fact that many of the Iconoclast sovereigns won from their subjects respect, and even popularity. The controversy continued for more than a hundred years : Irene temporarily restored the sacred pictures, and it was another Empress, Theodora, who, as regent for Michael III, secured the final victory of the Image-Worshippers (843). Woman and the monk at the long last carried the day. But history can now estimate the aims and achievements of the Iconoclast rulers with a less prejudiced judgment : we can see that they served Rome well. Leo saved Europe, Constantine V conquered the Bulgarians, Nicephorus reformed imperial finance, Theophilus endeavoured to render justice accessible to all. The architecture of the Image-Breakers might serve to exalt the prestige of a mortal emperor, their painting might turn to the representation of human pleasures and terrestrial pageantry, but at least we must be careful not to interpret their hostility to the sacred icons as inspired by any general opposition to art itself. In fine, the Iconoclasts gave to the Empire a new civil and military organisation (see ch. vii), they sought to adopt Roman law to the needs of their own day by the recognition of popular use and wont (see ch. xi), while they strove to check superstition and to free the civil power from the dictation of devout though narrow-minded monks (see ch. v). To that dictation History in her turn must refuse to bow.

PERIOD V. A.D. 867–1057

MACEDONIAN DYNASTY.

BASIL I, 867–886, was followed by his sons

LEO VI, 886–912 ⎫
ALEXANDER, 886–913 ⎭ though the paternity of Leo VI is doubtful. Alexander, nominally his colleague, did not rule, being entirely given up to pleasure, but acted for one year after Leo's death as guardian of the latter's son

CONSTANTINE VII (Porphyrogenitus), 912–959, who created his step-father Romanus I (Lecapenus) co-emperor in 919.

ROMANUS I, 919–944; but Romanus was overthrown with the help of his own sons in 944. Constantine VII was succeeded by his son

ROMANUS II, 959–963, on whose death his widow Theophano carried on the government for his infant sons

BASIL II, 963–1025,

CONSTANTINE VIII, 963–1025, sole ruler 1025–1028. Theophano married Nicephorus Phocas in 963, who reigned as

NICEPHORUS II, 963–969, until overthrown by a conspiracy of officers : he was succeeded by

JOHN I ZIMISKES, 969–976, who confined Theophano to a monastery. Constantine VIII on his death in 1028 left no sons, but three daughters

only, Eudoxia a nun, Theodora, who had no
wish for marriage, and Zoe. Following the
terms of the will of Constantine VIII, the
senator Romanus divorced his wife, married
Zoe and became Emperor as

ROMANUS III, 1028–1034. On his death Zoe
married her Paphlagonian lover, Michael, who
thus ascended the throne as

MICHAEL IV, 1034–1041. His nephew Michael was
made Cæsar and, when Michael IV died, Zoe
created him Emperor as

MICHAEL V, 1041–1042. When he imprisoned his
benefactress the people of Constantinople
rose in revolt and the two Basilian princesses

ZOE and ⎱ 1042, were together proclaimed as
THEODORA ⎰ joint sovereigns; but before two months had
passed Zoe (now 62 years of age) had married
again, and with her hand conferred the diadem
on her relative

CONSTANTINE IX MONOMACHUS, 1042–1054, she
herself dying in 1050. On the death of Constantine Theodora, the last of the princesses
" born in the purple," became sole ruler,

THEODORA, 1054–1056, and before her death
nominated as Emperor the general and
senator

MICHAEL STRATIOTIKOS, 1056–1057.

FIFTH PERIOD. 867–1057

In the year A.D. 800 Charlemagne had been
crowned by the Pope in Rome : from henceforth there were two Christian Empires.
Though the Emperor of the West might wish
to live in amity with his brother of East
Rome, yet a new factor of great moment had
thus been introduced into European politics—
the West possessed its civil as well as its

ecclesiastical head : Pope and Emperor were arrayed against Emperor and Patriarch. West and East were growing increasingly conscious that they now formed two sundered worlds; astride of the Iconoclast and Macedonian period stands the commanding figure of Photius, the Patriarch of Constantinople, who not only caused a temporary schism between the Churches of Old and New Rome, but formulated for all time those grounds of difference which served as pretext for the final breach in 1054. In these centuries Europe is seen in labour; one can watch how the fissure cleaving East and West extends, unevenly, but irresistibly. In the struggle of the converted Slavs for the retention of their vernacular liturgies those of the West fight a losing battle; the Roman Church with its Latin service triumphs, while Christian Bulgaria after brief hesitancy definitely falls to the Eastern side of the cleft (see ch. xiv). West and East only communicate through rare embassies : the threads of a common life are broken. For the Byzantine Court the Slav world is of primary importance, and behind the Bulgarian kingdom the West sinks below the horizon. To Constantine the Purple-born the princes of Bavaria and Saxony are rulers of the so-called Nemitz—the name which Slavs and Magyars gave to the Germans.

Within the Empire the second half of the ninth century is a period of recuperation : the Iconoclasts had been innovators, the new dynasty will rather gather up what can be saved of Rome's heritage, and from that legacy gain new strength. The law of Justinian is restored : knowledge is power, and thus Constantine VII, the Encyclopædist Emperor, formulates and codifies the principles which have made Rome great. The heroic struggles against Islam of the Bagratid sovereigns of Armenia had paved the way; thereafter with the rule of the born soldiers Nicephorus Phocas and John Zimiskes comes the great forward move. Syria and Mesopotamia are won from the Mohammedan, and even Antioch is recovered. The Byzantine Empire reaches its furthest limits. Basil II, the slayer of the Bulgars in long years of warfare, breaks the power of the kingdom which had been built up by the great Tsar Samuel. In 1014 of 15,000 blinded Bulgarians 150 alone were left a single eye to lead their comrades home. Vladimir Prince of Kiev is baptised and the conversion of Russia begins.

But with the death of Basil II Rome's greatness declined : the state fought unsuccessfully against the power of a territorial aristocracy and a Church which was ever absorbing more land for its monasteries and securing for this land immunity from civil burdens. Against the military nobles of Asia Court circles sought to hold their own by lessening the power of the army and thus weakening Rome's defences. The internal history of the Empire in the eleventh and twelfth centuries is thus dominated by the struggle between the capital and the provincial magnates.

PERIOD VI. A.D. 1057–1204

The dynastic sentiment for the Macedonian house having died with Theodora, her nominee is overthrown by the military nobility in favour of

ISAAC I COMNENUS, 1057–1059. Wearying of the hard task of empire, he abdicates, and nominates as Emperor his finance minister

CONSTANTINE X DUKAS, 1059–1067. On his death his widow Eudokia marries the General

ROMANUS IV DIOGENES, 1067–1071, who after his defeat by the Seljuk Turks at the battle of Manzikert (1071) is dethroned by Eudokia's stepson

MICHAEL VII DUKAS, 1071–1078, who is himself overthrown by a popular revolt, and is succeeded by

NICEPHORUS III BOTANIATES, 1078–1081. He was dethroned by a military rebellion which set on the throne Alexius Comnenus.

COMNENIAN DYNASTY.

ALEXIUS I COMNENUS (nephew of Isaac I), 1081–1118, inaugurated a period of restoration and reform; he was followed by his son

JOHN II, 1118–1143, who on his death was succeeded by his son

MANUEL, 1143–1180, for whose infant son

ALEXIUS II, 1180–1183, the Empress Maria and Alexius (a cousin of the Emperor) acted as regents. In 1183 Andronicus Comnenus (nephew of John II) was made colleague of Alexius II, and strangled the latter in the next year.

ANDRONICUS, 1183–1185, was overthrown by

ISAAC II, 1185–1195, head of the noble family of the Angeli, who was dethroned by his own brother

ALEXIUS III, 1195–1203; but the Crusaders restored

ISAAC II and
ALEXIUS IV } 1203–1204, until they were both deposed on the capture of Constantinople, 1204.

Sixth Period. 1057–1204

To summarise in a paragraph the history of this period is beyond the powers of the present writer; some of its problems must, however, be suggested. The new factor in the external situation was the appearance on the eastern frontier of the barbarous Seljukian Turks, who inflicted on Rome the terrible defeat of Manzikert (1071) from which the Empire never recovered. With revenues diminished, with much territory lost to the enemy or ravaged by their hordes, the task of maintaining the imperial forces was a matter of increasing difficulty; the Empire came to rely for its defence at sea on the navy of Venice. The support of Venice was bought only at the price of ruinous commercial concessions (cf. ch. xiii), and while within the State the civil and military parties fought for supremacy, the Western powers through the Crusades were at once attracted by the splendour and enraged by the diplomacy of the Byzantine Emperors. The Eastern Court might endeavour to purchase the armed help of the West by adroit promises of ecclesiastical union with the see of Peter, but the populace grew ever more hostile to Italian settlers and Western domination. To need protection and to loathe the only powers which can afford it is perhaps the supreme bitterness for a mighty empire. And for the men of the West who had found in the Promised Land so little milk, so little honey, so many a desert grave, who saw East Rome appropriating the spoils their arms had won, disillusion inflamed hate, and hate gave birth to jealous longing, and from malicious envy sprang the tragedy of the Empire's fall. A higher civilisation draws a lower irresistibly to itself. " The Crusades," a modern scholar has said, " are essentially a struggle for Constantinople." Is it really so?

SEVENTH PERIOD.   1204–1453

After the fall of the city a Latin Empire was established in the capital, and though the dynasty of the Lascarids ruled at Nicaea from 1206 to 1261, it was only in the latter year that under the Palæologi the Roman Empire was restored in Constantinople. The scope of this book renders it unnecessary to give the line of Emperors who reigned from 1261 to 1453. Hemmed in by the Serbian Kingdom on the West and by the Turks on the East, their realm was gradually reduced to the capital and the surrounding country, until at last the city itself was captured and the Roman Empire of the East was no more.

CHAPTER IV

BYZANTINE SOVEREIGNTY

The Empire and the Barbarians

And when the Queen of Sheba had seen all Solomon's wisdom, and the house that he had built, and the meat of his table, and the sitting of his servants, and the attendance of his ministers, and their apparel and his cupbearers, and his ascent by which he went up into the House of the Lord; there was no more spirit in her. And she said to the King, It was a true report that I heard in mine own land of thy acts and of thy wisdom. Howbeit I believed not the words, until I came, and my eyes had seen it : and, behold, the half was not told me : thy wisdom and prosperity exceedeth the fame which I heard. Happy are thy men, happy are these thy servants ! . . . Blessed be the Lord thy God, which delighteth in thee, to set thee on the throne of Israel : because the Lord loved Israel for ever, therefore made he thee king to do judgment and justice.—1 Kings x. 4–9.

SUCH were the sentiments of contemporary princes for Justinian and for many another Emperor of East Rome : the old Jewish chronicler wrote all unwittingly the finest commentary we possess upon Byzantine sovereignty. " How fair a Rule is monarchy, when God-sustained," thus George of Pisidia re-echoed the conviction of the subjects of Heraclius; and yet this Emperor in whom all authority was concentrated, is the successor of the Roman magistrate, and the heir of Octavian, the first citizen of the restored Republic.

When in the early days of Rome's history, the kingship had been overthrown, the royal prerogative was partitioned amongst many magistrates, while their tenure of power was in most cases shared with a colleague and limited to a brief period. Under the Empire the *imperium* of many of these magistrates was recalled, and the authority of each was placed in the hands of a single citizen; after some hesitation this cumulation of powers became the subject of a life-long grant. The Princeps controlled the army and those provinces which needed military protection; elsewhere the republican magistrates retained their old rights. Augustus might honestly seek to make the senate an active partner in the work of administration, but the senate refused to play its part, and reluctantly the Emperor was forced to assume new duties: thus the imperial burden grew. When Tiberius retired in weariness to Capri, it was realised that the organs of the old republican state were no longer equal to the increased strain: as soon as the Emperor refused to shoulder the load, confusion resulted. Under Claudius was built up an administrative staff, formed of the Emperor's freedmen, working independently of, but side by side with, the old magistracies of Rome: the servants of the household of Cæsar stepped into the place

of the old constitutional executive, and before
these imperial bureaux the state capitulated.
In the reign of Hadrian citizens from the ranks
of the middle classes (the equestrian order) were
substituted for the Emperor's freedmen : the
domestic bureaux of Cæsar became branches
of the civil service of Rome. Thus the Senate,
which from the beginning of the Principate
had tended to become a sleeping partner,
gradually took up the position of a partner
with limited liability, having no effective
control over the policy of the State.

The attempt of the senate in the third
century to reassert its privileges was fore-
doomed to failure. Senators were excluded
from the army by Gallienus, and from the provincial administration by Diocletian, and the
middle classes triumphed over the aristocracy.
But with the restoration of imperial authority
under the successors of Diocletian the senators
were no longer rivals of the monarch, and the
house of Constantine could open the administration to the whole strength of the Empire,
knights and senators could alike be enlisted
in the service of a common master who held
all power in his own hands. The civil and
military careers were, as we have seen (cf.
ch. i), sharply separated, but the two sides
of the divided *imperium* were united in the
Imperator; the old legislative assemblies of
the people met no longer, for the people only
exercised their sovereignty in successive acts of
abdication—by their choice of an Emperor
they surrendered to him their inherited

supremacy : their delegate was source of law, and his mandatories were its interpreters. Under the Republic things profane and things divine had alike been subject to the magistrate's *imperium*—the priest was but the counsellor in matters of religion—so now the old Roman theory lived on in New Rome : the Emperor as Pontifex Maximus was Head of the Church, Defender of the Faith. Though the scruples of Gratian might cause him to refuse the Pagan title, a Christian Emperor still owed a double duty to his subjects—the care of the soul as well as of the body : religion even under the changed conditions was not solely the concern of the individual citizen : it was still a part of State policy (cf. ch. v). From the outset the Emperor had been something more than a mere man—Octavius chose the title of Augustus because of the associations of the word with divinity : in life, it was true, he was not yet a God, whatever subjects in the Eastern provinces, long used to God-kings, might make of him, but in death he dropped that in him which was less than Godhead, and the decree of the senate assured the Roman world that another Olympian had taken his place amongst the Immortals. The Christian Emperor in his turn it would seem rose at his death to a similar position in the Paradise of the new faith, and sat " to bear joint rule with the Son of God " in celestial places—in life he was like unto God, in death he became " of sacred memory." But despite such traces of the older idea as occur in

Ambrose's funeral speech on Valentinian, or in the epigram on the tomb of Theodosius II, in general beatification takes the place of apotheosis. To these inherited Roman elements, however, there were added new Eastern features. The third century had seen the spread of Oriental influences in the Roman world, and the Persian conception of kingship as the gift of God was grafted on to the Roman theory of the *imperium* of the magistrate : the Emperor became a being unapproachable, sacrosanct; in his presence men prostrated themselves before the Vice-gerent of High Heaven. The first citizen now wore the diadem of the monarch, and everything associated with his person acquired from that association a sacred character. But it is important to realise that even this development has its roots in a long past : it is but the triumph of that view of the Emperor's position which the Hellenistic East had from the first tended to adopt, but which had been discouraged by the Roman standpoint held by most of the earlier Cæsars. Diocletian explicitly claimed those honours which in former days had only been accorded to a Caligula or a Domitian. It is easy to exaggerate the break with the past in the transformation of the Empire effected by Diocletian and Constantine.

So much it was necessary to say by way of introduction, but when we have seen that the government of the East Roman Emperors was an autocracy, two questions at once suggest themselves : what was the source of the autocrat's power ? what were the forces which conditioned its exercise ? The title to the throne continued to be elective throughout the history of the Empire; the ruler was chosen by senate and army exercising their inherited rights as king-makers, and their choice was confirmed by the populace : either senate or army (in practice a portion of the army representing the sum of Rome's military forces) could nominate a candidate, and the other body would concur : thus the steps in the making of an Emperor are (i) proclamation by senate or army giving the nominee " a presumptive constitutional status which the event might either confirm or annul " (ii) concurrence in this proclamation by the other authority possessing this right of nomination, (iii) ratification of the choice so made by acclamation of the Roman people assembled (usually) in the Hebdomon, and (iv) coronation with the diadem, usually, but not necessarily, by the œcumenical Patriarch, as representing *the electors*, but not the Church.

This is the procedure for the delegation of sovereignty so far as constitutional practice is concerned, yet this procedure can only give a human title : but the Emperor's throne rests upon far surer foundations, he is the Anointed of God ; chosen from his birth to fulfil the will of Heaven, the successful candidate for the throne is thus of necessity the Lord's elect. It matters not by what means he won his triumph : success is in itself his justification ;

thereby his past is obliterated, on this in the last resort he founds his claim to be obeyed. The autocracy is thus a royal priesthood, the Emperor himself is counted amongst the clergy, and when presenting the offering which custom prescribes, he can enter the sanctuary, approach the altar where none of the laity may pass, and can even kiss the altar cloth and take in his hands the consecrated bread. To the Emperor as to Peter of old was confided the shepherding of the flock of Christ. To mark more clearly this priestly side of his office there was added perhaps as early as the ninth century a further symbolic act to the coronation ceremony—the Patriarch anointed the Emperor with consecrated oil; here he was not expressing the will of the State, but the will of the Deity. This theory of the basis of sovereignty carried with it a further consequence : who is man that he should circumscribe the will of Heaven?—the Lord of Hosts took David from the sheepcote, from following the sheep to be ruler over His people, over Israel : and to the East Roman, as to the Hebrew Psalmist, it was true that promotion cometh neither from the East, nor from the West, nor from the South, but God is the judge : he putteth down one and setteth up another— therefore the imperial throne was open to all, to peasant and aristocrat, to unlearned and learned alike, the only condition was that the ruler was a Christian, and later that he was an orthodox Christian—for great or small, rich or poor, he might yet be God's chosen.

c

The Emperor once elected, there was no constitutional method by which he might be deposed, save by a successful revolution; and here again the fact of success set the seal of Heaven's approval upon him who, had he failed, would have been merely a usurper. Jehovah had transferred his favour from Saul to David, and so now God could withdraw his support from the ruler. Thus revolution itself is legitimated and becomes part of the constitutional practice : " Roman government," says Mommsen, " was an autocracy tempered by the legal right of revolution."

But an elective succession in a state where usurpation is only treason, if unsuccessful, while it may tend to safeguard imperial efficiency, gives to the subject no surety for ordered government. And thus the theory was itself modified to this extent : the delegation of sovereignty to the Emperor was held to give him the right to crown his own successor during his lifetime, and though he, while living, kept in his own hands the supreme power, on his death that power would automatically pass to his delegate : the right of choice was thus taken from the electors : they had but to greet the new ruler : " the King is dead, long live the King ! " Indeed, periodically in Byzantine history a strong dynastic sentiment manifests itself : in the fourth century it finds constant expression in the panegyrists on behalf of the house of Constantine; it appears again in the seventh for the family of Heraclius, and yet again in favour of the descendants of Basil and in the case of the Comneni. It was this dynastic sentiment which brought women to the imperial throne, for there was no Salic law in the Eastern Empire. But the really interesting point to notice is that this hereditary devotion to a royal family was never allowed to prejudice the safety of the State, for when under the Basilian monarchs a student Emperor, as Constantine VII, ascended the throne, a soldier was appointed as his colleague to fight the battles of the Empire, for New Rome remained a military state, and most of her great Emperors were also great soldiers. As Synesius said at the end of the fourth century, their Greek title Autocrator represented the Latin Imperator, the leader of armies,[1] and the true position of the Emperor was still in the midst of his soldiery; however insistently a bureaucracy might represent that it was the ruler's duty to stay in the capital, and not to court danger on active service, a strong Emperor could always disregard the prohibition and lead his troops to battle. Maurice in the sixth century might yield to the view of his advisers, Heraclius in the seventh appealed to the Roman army, and found in them a force which followed him gladly into the heart of Persia. When the Emperor Michael allowed an abbot to dictate his military policy, he was dethroned by the

[1] At a later date it acquired a special meaning, and is used to describe the plenitude of power of a superior over his inferior colleagues.

Armenian Leo. It is indeed their capacity as leaders of men which is the outstanding feature of the long line of East Roman sovereigns.

We have seen then that the government was an autocracy—that all power exercised within the Roman Empire was derived from the Emperor as its source—but this is an inadequate statement of Roman imperial theory: the Emperor—the King (Basileus), as he was officially styled after the fall of the Persian Empire, whose sovereign had alone disputed with him the title—was no mere ruler of the provinces subject to Rome. As Christ had claimed the world for His inheritance, so His Vice-gerent must embrace the world in his sway: he too is a world saviour, his is the power that maintains the world—he is the universal sovereign, who has rights of pre-eminence over all lands. Those lands may be in the possession of German princes or conquered by the infidel, but the German prince is Rome's delegate, the infidel only occupies Rome's territory on sufferance, and ultimately the true owner will resume possession.

And not only so : as the earthly empire is formed in the likeness of the heavenly, so it is not only universal but eternal; man cannot overthrow it. Bad emperors are but God's scourges, and when the time of chastisement is over, if God's people repent of their sins, the sun of his favour will shine again. Thus the Christian faith becomes for the state a constant well-spring of regeneration. The promise of Jupiter to the Romans—

His ego nec metas rerum nec tempora pono,
Imperium sine fine dedi—

One greater than Jupiter had confirmed; what
might have been a mere political aspiration had
become transformed into a religious dogma.

To this world-wide claim of domination what
then are the theoretical or practical limitations? In the first place, though the
Emperor is supreme legislator, though there
is no human authority to call him to account,
yet for that very reason, as Agapetus the deacon
warns Justinian, he should constrain himself
to observe the laws, and Basil I acknowledged
this obligation. The Emperor is further
surrounded by men trained in the conservative
traditions of a highly complicated bureaucracy: the senate, save when it exercises
its old power of king-making, has become a
council of administrators, men who preferred
well-trodden paths. When Proclus successfully dissuaded Anastasius from adopting the
son of the Persian king, he began his advice
to the Emperor by the words "I have never
learned to accustom myself to innovations,
and I fear them above everything else, for I
know full well that in making innovations
safety can in no way be preserved." There
must have been many a Proclus in Byzantine
history, whose counsel the sovereign found it
prudent to adopt. Again, at least until the
seventh century, the populace of the capital
with its city militia was a very real power,
ready if thwarted of its will to break into riot,
to put forward a rival candidate to the throne,

and to spread confusion by arson and assassination. When, as it would seem, organised popular resistance to the imperial will was broken under the Heraclian house, it was the monks who, as the new tribunes of the people, ventured to oppose the Emperors; they could rely on the support of the faithful, and were more dangerous adversaries than the Patriarch whom the sovereign might depose. Nor did the army fail to use its power to put a rude stop to measures of which it disapproved: it was the stern military discipline of Maurice in the sixth century which cost him throne and life. But beyond these obvious checks there remained the subtle influence of a tradition which expected from its rulers *philanthropia*, a word which defies translation, but which sums up the century-long conception of the Emperor's duty of large humane service to his subjects—a conception in which there still lingered the old Roman view of office as entailing obligation, rather than as conferring a personal privilege. Through Themistius (fourth century) Agapetus (sixth century) and George of Pisidia (seventh century), to mention no others, there is an insistence on the ruler's obligation to show this love of humanity, and this ideal cannot but have exercised a restraining force.

Finally, before their grant of the imperial power the electors would exact an express pledge from their delegate. Thus the senate required from Anastasius I an oath that he would administer the Empire conscientiously,

and not visit offences upon anyone with whom
he had a quarrel, and, his orthodoxy being
suspect, he was also, on the demand of the
Patriarch, compelled to sign a written oath
that he would introduce no novelty into the
Church. In course of time, the precise date
is uncertain, the sovereign on his coronation
regularly took a formal oath, which began
with a confession of orthodox faith and contained a confirmation of the decrees of the
seven œcumenical and other local councils,
and of the rights and privileges of the Church.
The Emperor then proceeded to promise that
he would remain a true servant, son and
defender of Holy Church, that he would be
" philanthropic " towards his subjects, would
uphold justice, and would, so far as possible,
abstain from the infliction of mutilations or
of the death penalty. The form of the oath
is interesting as showing what the Byzantines
required of their monarch.

But the Byzantine Emperor was the centre
of a Court and within his palace his actions
were controlled and prescribed by the rigid
dictates of court ceremonial. Since this
ceremonial code was itself a part of Byzantine
policy of state, we may close this chapter by
a brief consideration of Byzantine diplomacy.

No more typically Byzantine work has been
preserved to us than the treatise *De Ceremoniis*,
in which the Emperor Constantine Porphyrogenitus committed to his son the secrets of
the etiquette of the East Roman Court. Here
in minutest detail is described the part taken

by every rank of the imperial hierarchy in the long course of the receptions and processions which made up the Byzantine " Christian year." Dress, gesture, place, time, formal words hallowed by immemorial custom—all are specified. From the " Gothic Games " at Christmas, when men in masks with shield and lance in the midst of the demesmen of the Circus parties went through their strange dance, and uttered incomprehensible words which still perplex the philologist; through the festival of the Brumalia—a heritage from pagan times—when a feast was celebrated on successive days for every letter of the alphabet, and the guests, chosen according to the initial letter of their names, received handsome presents from the Emperor; through weddings, birthdays, baptisms, coronations, triumphs, burials and court mournings, through church services and public processions we can follow this unceasing pageant of an Emperor's days.

Picture for a moment the arrival of a barbarian chieftain from steppe or desert in this Byzantine Court. He has been royally entertained, under the vigilant care of imperial officials he has seen the wonders of the capital, and to-day he is to have audience with the Emperor. Through a dazzling maze of marble corridors, through chambers rich with mosaic and cloth of gold, through long lines of palace guards in white uniforms, amidst patricians, bishops, generals and senators, to the music of organs and church choirs he

passes, supported by eunuchs, until at last
oppressed with interminable splendour he
falls prostrate in the presence of the silent,
motionless, hieratic figure of the Lord of New
Rome, the heir of Constantine, seated on the
throne of the Cæsars : before he can rise,
Emperor and throne have been caught aloft, and
with vestments changed since last he gazed
the sovereign looks down upon him, surely as
God regarding mortal men. Who is he, as he
hears the roar of the golden lions that surround
the throne or the song of the birds on the
trees, who is he that he should decline the
Emperor's behests ? He stays not to think
of the mechanism which causes the lions to
roar or the birds to sing : he can scarce
answer the questions of the logothete speaking
for his imperial master : his allegiance is won :
he will fight for the Roman Christ and his
Empire. He receives honours and decorations
and subsidies for his promised defence of the
frontiers—perhaps he may be accorded a
place in the official hierarchy, become a
Patrician or Master of the Soldiery—even
perchance, if his help is of great consequence
to the Empire, be promised a Byzantine
princess in marriage, as was the Chazar chief
by Heraclius. He will accept Christianity,
the Emperor will even stand as his godfather
at the sacred font, and henceforth a bishop
subject to the Patriarch of Constantinople
and East Roman clergy will sustain the interest
of Romania in his land. Should he be overthrown by his own people he has an asylum

assured him whence he may be restored by Roman arms : his loyalty will be yet more unquestioned. Though the Empire did not maintain permanent representatives at foreign courts, missions will pass and repass, and in the imperial chancery their reports will be stored, and the diplomacy of East Rome will be guided by first-hand information upon the internal resources and conditions of all the neighbouring barbarian kingdoms; each will hold the other in check. Chazars will fight the battles of Heraclius against Persia, and in after years hold the neighbouring Patzinaks in check, while the Empire will maintain communications with the Chazars through the City of Cherson and will even build for them their frontier town of Sarkel on the Sea of Azov. If the Chazars prove unruly the Alans of the Caucasus are ready to invade their land at the Emperor's bidding. In the sixth century Lombards and Avars conquer the Gepids, just as later Russians and Patzinaks are summoned to attack the Bulgars, and are only too successful. Thus Rome maintained the balance of power amongst the peoples that encircled her.

The Empire of East Rome has fallen, but her ceremonial still lives : the ecclesiastic has taken the place of the civil ruler : and while the Greek monk bows prostrate before the Patriarch of Constantinople, just as men once bowed before the Emperor, the Pope in S. Peter's has inherited the pageantry which once surrounded the autokrator—the " Equal of the Apostles."

CHAPTER V

THE ORTHODOX CHURCH

We do not change the boundaries marked out by
our fathers : we keep the tradition we have received.
We beseech, therefore, the people of God, the faithful flock, to hold fast to the ecclesiastical traditions.
The gradual taking away of what has been handed
down to us would be undermining the foundation
stones, and would in no short time overthrow the
whole structure.—S. John Damascene on Holy
Images (translated by Mary H. Allies, pp. 54 and 71.
London, 1898).

IT is not only the ceremonial of East Rome
which survives : the Orthodox Church remains
and even to-day preserves much of that
character which it acquired under the Christian
Emperors. Its theology, its rites and liturgies,
its saints and its festivals, the form of monastic
piety and asceticism are all a heritage from
Byzantine days, treasured with inflexible
conservatism. Here more obviously than
elsewhere the study of early Christianity
explains the religious conditions of our own
time.

Under Constantine, as we have seen, the
Church of the Catacombs became the Church
Triumphant; the capital of the Roman world
was a Christian City. But Constantinople

remained subject as regards ecclesiastical jurisdiction to the bishop of Heraclea. The internal history of the Church after its recognition by the State is thus dominated by the efforts of the bishop of Constantinople to assert on the one hand his independence of the Metropolitan of Heraclea and on the other his supremacy over his rival of Alexandria. In both struggles the patriarch of New Rome was victorious, and in his victory the Emperor shared : Justinian stands as priest-king at the head of the Church, and in the priest-king's capital are centred the Church's life and organisation. It is essential to outline this development.

In Constantinople, formed after the model of the earlier Rome, possessing its senate and city-prefect (since 359), was centralised the civil administration of the Empire. In the eastern provinces of the Empire the organisation of the Church had come to be modelled on that of the civil jurisdiction. S. Paul with the eye of a general had chosen provincial capitals as the strategic points in the conquest of the world for Christ; these were the fortresses which must at all costs be captured : here it was in especial that the early Church came face to face with that system of Emperor-worship which was its great idolatrous abomination : here was Satan's seat. Thus, naturally, as the new religion spread, the country congregations looked up to the bishop of the city as their head. When Diocletian changed the civil provincial organisation, the ecclesiastical organisation was also refashioned. In the East for Church and State the administrative unit was one and the same. Foundation by an apostle was the criterion by which the West determined the claim of any bishopric to precedence; the East sought to justify an organisation which was the result of a long historical development : it found that justification in the theory that it was a city's position in the civil hierarchy which decided its precedence in the ecclesiastical sphere. Centuries later Byzantium sought to overtrump Rome herself on her own ground; the older capital claimed S. Peter for founder : New Rome discovered on the faith of a timely forgery that she could trace her title back to S. Andrew, the Apostle who had brought Peter first to Christ. But the earlier theory finds explicit recognition in the canons of the second œcumenical council, held at Constantinople in 381, which gave the first place in the Eastern Church, directly after the see of Rome, to the bishop of the capital " *because Constantinople is New Rome.*" The claim of the upstart see might not be acknowledged by Rome until the days of Innocent III (1198–1216), but the step was taken once for all, and the city of the Emperors had won its freedom from the jurisdiction of Heraclea. A later application of the same principle determined in the ninth century the question whether Bulgaria was to owe allegiance to Pope or Patriarch (see p. 223).

The subsequent contests within the Church

sprang ultimately from the determination
of the bishops of Alexandria to maintain their
influence and authority against the rising
power of Constantinople. Egypt since the
time of Julius Cæsar had always occupied an
exceptional position within the Empire, and
had never become an organic part of the
provincial system. Its one great centre,
alike for trade and culture, was Alexandria :
the Metropolis was without a rival, while
suffragan bishops and provincial clergy could
assert no real independence. Egypt was still
a nation, and the old kingship was but transformed : the Patriarch, as a spiritual Pharaoh,
was enthroned in the capital; he was the
representative of a people and for them his
word was law; from the desert, populous with
anchorites, he could call forth his armies,
and the monkish hosts, wielding their clubs,
were ever ready to obey his summons.
Alexandria fought a battle with a double
front, seeking to assert her freedom alike of
old Rome on the Tiber and of the New Rome
on the Bosphorus, though from time to time
policy might dictate a temporary alliance with
one foe in order to secure a triumph over the
other. The struggle must be briefly illustrated.

In the fourth century Alexandria established
her prestige by her defence of the true faith
against Arian heretics; the end hallows the
means, and contemporaries were ready, if
need be, to forgive Athanasius everything for
his championship of orthodoxy. When the
council of 381 conferred pre-eminence in the

East on the see of Constantinople, Egypt was not slow to take up the challenge.

But for some time Constantinople played into the hands of Egypt; although Eutropius, the eunuch chamberlain of Arcadius, might carry in Alexandria's despite the election of Chrysostom as bishop of New Rome (397), the outspoken criticism of the great moralist offended the Empress Eudoxia and the court; Theophilus, the Egyptian patriarch, secured his rival's banishment, and the protests of the West passed unheeded.   When the next battle was fought, the victorious Cyril was bishop of Alexandria, while Nestorius, trained in the historical and critical methods of the school of Antioch, was Patriarch of Constantinople (elected 428); the latter was accused of dividing the personality of Christ into the divine Word (Logos) and the human Jesus, and at the third œcumenical council of Ephesus (431) Cyril, acting as Papal legate, secured his condemnation and deposition.   Theodosius II after some hesitation yielded to the commanding personality of the Egyptian bishop. Alexandria triumphed afresh.   But Rome grew uneasy, and Pope Leo I demanded of Cyril's successor, Dioscorus, that he should submit to the control of the see of Peter : this claim determined the policy of the patriarch; in a theological age he sought by a victory in the most important sphere—the realm of dogma—to win at one and the same time ecclesiastical independence and political domination.

The monk Eutyches in attacking Nestorius had maintained that there was in Christ not only a unity of personality, but a single nature, and was in consequence charged with heresy. At the " Robber Synod " of Ephesus (449) Dioscorus, supported by the imperial favour, secured in a packed assembly the condemnation of Flavian, bishop of Constantinople, the principal accuser of Eutyches, and Flavian was succeeded by Anatolius, a partisan of Dioscorus. Pope and Western Emperor petitioned Theodosius in vain. Alexandria had won the day : her patriarch was all powerful.

What were the factors which two years later at the Council of Chalcedon (451) brought about the condemnation of the doctrine of Eutyches, the banishment of Dioscorus and the close of Alexandrian dictation ? There is no doubt that, though the city populace of the Egyptian capital remained loyal to their patriarch, his own clergy were weary of the arbitrary treatment which they had suffered at his hands, while other Churches refused to tolerate longer his tyrannous overlordship.

But more important still was the death of Theodosius II (A.D. 450); his successor, elected through the influence of Pulcheria, was no longer willing to champion the claims of Alexandria. He and his virgin wife were determined to assert the authority of the throne, and anxiously sought to restore religious concord throughout the Churches of the East. Marcian was prepared, it would seem, to come to terms with Dioscorus, but the latter, he insisted, must make concessions. This the Patriarch refused to do : either Alexandria must win an unconditional triumph, or he would relinquish the struggle and earn the martyr's crown. Basil of Seleucia put the case quite clearly at Chalcedon: " Dioscorus would have all the bishops go into banishment on his behalf : this saint claims to fight for the true faith, but he values his person above God, above the sees of Rome, Constantinople and Antioch, and above all the other bishops. If Alexandria is defeated and Dioscorus dies, still the world will not remain without a bishop." Pope and Emperor demanded that the pride of Egypt should be broken : the Patriarch would not yield, and thus himself brought about his own deposition and exile. The Council of Chalcedon meant the triumph of Constantinople, and the victory of centralising tendencies within the Eastern Church.

The Council had accepted the Western formula elaborated in the dogmatic letter or Tomos of Leo the Great : two natures, the divine and the human, were to be recognised in Christ even after His incarnation, their difference being preserved despite the unity of person. The trend of Alexandrian theology, always inclined to mysticism and allegory, was so to accentuate the divinity of Christ that His humanity was obscured : the divine nature swallowed up the human, and the

Church of Egypt was thus led to the doctrine of a single divine nature—monophysitism. The party which ultimately formed the independent monophysite Church was united in its resistance to the definition of 451 and in its rejection of the Tomos of Leo. The Council of Chalcedon brought not peace, but a sword. We have already noticed the political problem which thus faced the Roman Emperors : how could they placate the opposition of Syria and Egypt passionately espousing heresy, and at the same time maintain communion with the orthodox West ? Zeno's Henoticon of 482 united the Eastern Churches, but the price was schism with Rome (484). Throughout the reign of Anastasius (at heart a monophysite) this breach was unhealed : Justin restored communion with the West, but under Justinian Jacobus Baradaeus founded the independent Jacobite Church. The Heraclian house once more sought to effect a union with the monophysites, but the doctrines of a single theandric energy or of a single will in the incarnate Christ were of no permanent avail, and it was only with the loss of the heretical lands of Syria and Egypt to the Mohammedans that the problem ceased to vex imperial statesmanship. The Empire could now afford to be orthodox : Justinian II made his peace with Rome.

When the other patriarchates of the Roman East had become bishoprics *in partibus infidelium,* the Patriarch of Constantinople remained without a rival : his jurisdiction at length became conterminous with the Empire. But the patriarch of the capital lived under the shadow of the imperial palace. Constantine had been at once the first Christian emperor and the restorer of the supremacy of the Roman state. When he came to Constantinople he had already learned by the failure of the bishops of the West to solve the Donatist problem that he could no longer leave to the ecclesiastical authorities the unguided government of the Church. The emperor who summoned and directed as its President the Council of Nicaea (A.D. 325) pointed the way which was followed by his successors, and no Patriarch of New Rome could long withstand the imperial will or withdraw himself from imperial dictation. Thus in the triumph of Chalcedonian orthodoxy and the triumph of centralisation ended the struggle for supremacy within the Eastern Church.

The sixth century indeed had seen the last great attack on the paganism which still existed within the Empire. A parallel stream of legislation had for more than 200 years been directed against heretics on the one hand and pagans on the other. Constantine had repressed with violence the Donatists of Africa, though rather as disturbers of the public peace than as misbelievers : Constantius and Valens endeavoured to enforce Arianism. But it was left to Theodosius I to take the decisive measures; he was in consequence given the title of " the Great " by an enthusiastic Church. Heretics were no longer to be ordained and were banished from Constantinople, while Manichæans and Eunomians were deprived of the power to bequeath and the right to receive legacies. Theodosius II extended the disability to all sects. Eunomians under Theodosius the Great might neither hold office at court nor in the army, while an edict of Theodosius the Younger declared all heretics to be incapacitated for military service. Justinian whose ideas of government were summed up in the brief formula, " One state, one law, one church " was even more severe. Heretics though subject to all the burdens of citizenship could enjoy none of its privileges : under his legislation they were debarred from entering any of the professions, their churches were to be destroyed, their assemblies were forbidden ; their evidence against the orthodox might not be received in the law courts, and they were unable to make a will, to take under a testamentary disposition or to inherit property on an intestacy. The heretic became a social outcast, while Justinian's policy in the special case of the Manichæans was one of simple extermination : the interests of the immortal soul outweighed those of the perishable body, and all chance of infection must be ruthlessly removed.

Another line of statutes was directed against paganism. Constantine, it is asserted, issued a general prohibition of sacrifices, public as well as private, and directed that fallen temples should not be rebuilt. Constantius ordered the temples to be closed " that the possibility of sin might be taken from the lost." Theodosius the Great forbad any worshipper to enter a temple, while in 392 sacrifice was put on the same footing as treason and thus entailed confiscation of the offender's property. Even the cult of the Lares and Penates—the deities of the home—was declared illegal. In 416 Theodosius II banished all pagans from the civil or military service of the Empire, and in a rescript a few years later the sovereign could state " we believe that the pagans are no more." The wish must here have been father to the thought, for in the sixth century there were still thousands within the Empire whom John of Ephesus dragooned into Christianity.

In 496 it needed two startling miracles to induce the inhabitants of Edessa to forgo the celebration of their nocturnal feast of lights—the reader should turn to the account given by Joshua the Stylite of these pagan revels (Wright's translation, pp. 18–21)—but some eighty years later in the capital when it was feared that Anatolius of Antioch, accused of having taken part in a sacrifice, might be acquitted through the influence of his friends the populace burst into revolt : bishop and Emperor, men shouted, were betraying the faith, and order was not restored until the offender had been mangled by wild beasts in the amphitheatre, then impaled, and finally devoured by wolves. After this exemplary punishment we hear no more of heathenism in Constantinople, while the closing by Justinian of the University of Athens sounded the death knell of pagan philosophy.

From the first the effect of this legislation had been to produce many conversions, but all too often the fear of these new adherents towards the Christian God was taught by the precept of men and their hearts remained far removed, retaining their allegiance to the older faith. There was many a fourth-century Vicar of Bray whose supple convictions enabled him to enjoy the sunshine of imperial favour, whether his master were an orthodox Christian, Arian heretic or, as Julian the Apostate, a pagan zealot. Thus moral and religious standards within the Church sank rapidly. Men felt that the Christian life was losing its rigorous ideal, and they strove to break away from a world which was too much with them. The wastes of Egypt were peopled with solitaries, seeking communion with their God. They did not actively sever themselves from the organised Church, as the Montanists and the earlier Puritans had done, but they were self-sufficient; they did not need the Church's ministrations. Monasticism thus stood apart from the Church: it was in one respect an individualistic protest against an institution which had paid too heavy a price for state support. But if the Church was centralising authority in her

internal government, she was none the less
determined that no religious movement should
remain out of relation to herself : every new
form of piety should champion her cause, and
if accommodation were needed, she was ready
to employ a timely economy whereby to gain
her ends. If, however, the new passion for
asceticism was to be brought under her control,
it must be regulated. The solitary must be
brought into touch with a community of those
who shared his ideals, and thus given scope
for the exercise of the Christian virtues.
This was the work of Eustathius of Sebasteia
and of Basil the Great. The latter sought to
found asceticism on a scriptural basis : the
ascetic is one who walks in accordance with
the Gospel of Jesus, who " practises with a
view to perfection and trains himself by means
of solitude, renunciation and continence for
the attainment of the one great prize, union
with God." To Basil the life of the solitary
was inactive and unfruitful, and labour in the
field or workshop was to form part of the life
of prayer. The rules of Basil served as a
model to S. Benedict when legislating for the
monks of the West.

But after all it was the holy eremite dwelling
in the lonely cavern or on the precipitous cliff
who awoke the wondering awe and passionate
enthusiasm of the common folk. Pilgrims
came from West and East to catch a sight of
the stylite saint who had spent long years
upon his pillar until he could stand no longer
and could only rest against the side of the

framework which surrounded him.[1] Once
more the Church sought to turn this popular
devotion to its own purposes, and the usurper
Basiliscus was forced to relinquish heresy at
the sight of the swollen-footed Daniel tottering
into his presence from the pillar which only
this supreme menace to the faith had induced
him to desert. The bishop who waited through
the scorching heat of a long summer day
imploring the stylite saint to let down his
ladder to receive ordination, and who at last
read the ordination service from the pillar's
foot despite the saint's protestations, though
he could lay no hands upon the recusant's
head, is a figure of the Church which claimed
every movement for her own, and would embrace every influence which might strengthen
her hold upon the life and thought of the
Empire.

And the pilgrim returning carried with him
as we have seen (p. 33) an image or picture
of the saint, and this practice may have
served to reinforce that worship of images
which was to give rise to the long-protracted
Iconoclast controversy.

The heart of the Empire in the eighth
and ninth centuries was to be found in Asia
Minor and Armenia, where Puritan influences
were still strong : here was the home of the

---

[1] It is probable that the original motive for this
form of Christian asceticism was to render any freedom of movement impossible. There is no reason to
suppose any direct connection with earlier forms of
pagan asceticism.

Paulicians who hated monkery, and protested against the superstitious practices and rites of the Church, and hence came the Iconoclast Emperors. With them sided the Army, mainly drawn from Asia Minor and Armenia, a large proportion of the civil service and many of the bishops. For the icons fought European Greece and the monasteries.

Unfortunately, since the writings of the Iconoclasts have perished, we can only reconstruct the grounds of their attack upon image worship from the treatises of their opponents. We can, however, at least see that the Image-Breakers are not rationalists, as they have sometimes been represented, but religious reformers : the reverence paid to the sacred pictures seemed to them idolatrous and degrading. Popular devotion was indeed prepared to go to great lengths, it would even choose an icon to be god-parent to a child. The imperial party considered as blasphemous the attempt to represent the Divine in human form or to figure the mysteries of the spirit world through the medium of matter. Were not perchance the conquests of the Arabs, the haters of images, a judgment of an outraged Heaven?

The Image-Worshippers were not less sincere : to many it is true the fight may have been a struggle for subsistence : like the worthy craftsmen of the city of Ephesus, they felt as painters of sacred pictures that their trade was endangered, but to others profounder issues were at stake. Some of the

Iconodules were still content to employ the argument for images which had been used in the East as early as the fourth century and was later also adopted in the West—the sacred pictures were to form the Bible of the uneducated : the image is a memorial, it speaks to the sight as words to the ear, it brings understanding. But it is not merely that the icon can teach and give fresh courage, it is a far deeper line of argument which underlies the defence of the Image-Worshippers ; to them for the human mind to endeavour to forgo the help of corporeal things is presumption : the attempt is doomed to failure from the first, for the invisible things of God since the creation of the world are made visible through images. Everything has a double significance, corporeal and spiritual : soul is shrouded by the veil of body, with the bodily ear we listen to physical words, and thereby understand spiritual truths. Baptism is double—of water and the spirit—so is communion and prayer and psalmody. For this reason Christ took a body and a soul. In fact the Iconoclast hatred of images, they argued, is based upon a particular view of matter : for them matter is evil. But this implies an impossible Manichæan dualism : Christ by becoming flesh has sanctified—has deified—matter; to hold that Christ cannot duly be represented through the medium of matter is thus really to deny the Incarnation, to strike at the very heart and centre of the Christian hope. It is not matter which we adore : it is the Lord of matter, becoming matter for our sake, taking up His abode in matter, and working out our salvation through matter. No, matter is not despicable, nothing that comes from God is despicable : only man's invention—sin—is despicable. Matter is endued with a divine power through prayer made to those who are depicted in image; by itself matter is of no account, but if the one presented in image be full of grace, men become partakers of his grace according to their faith. As S. Basil wrote " Honouring the image leads to the prototype." In sum the Iconodule contended : if you do not worship images, you do not worship the Son of God, who is Himself the living Image of the invisible God.

The Worshippers of Images triumphed and the sacred pictures remained. It is usually stated that as a result of the struggle statuary was banished from the house of God. It may be questioned, however, whether there is satisfactory evidence for any widespread use of statues in the Churches of the Eastern Empire even before the Iconoclastic controversy.

But in its second stage the Iconoclast controversy assumed a political character; it has even been suggested that in this later period persecution was confined to Constantinople : the Emperor would be master in his own capital. For the monks were not only defending images, and thus championing ecclesiastical tradition, they were in their own way revolutionaries; they were fighting for a new freedom, and striving to break down the relation between State and Church as it had long been established in the Byzantine world. For the Emperor of East Rome was not only defender of the faith : he was the head of the Church : the heir of Constantine the Great ; he alone could summon a Church Council, the religious parliament of the Empire, where procedure was modelled on that of the secular senate, where the gospel took the place of the pagan altar of victory : his lay commissioners presided at the sessions of the council, and its conclusions had no force until authority was given to them by the Emperor's approval. In time even these representative assemblies appeared dangerously democratic, and the autocrat of Constantinople defined the dogmas of the Church by imperial edict. The bishop of the court was in fact appointed by the Emperor, who could enforce his will in religious matters by the deposition of a recalcitrant patriarch. His subjects hailed Justinian as priest-king, and it was his bishop that gave classical expression to the theory of Cæsaropapism in the words " Nothing should happen in the Church against the command and will of the Emperor."

It was this theory of the relation between Church and State which was attacked by Theodore of the monastery of Studios and the later Iconodules. They would give to Cæsar that which is Cæsar's and to God that which is God's. S. John Damascene thus formulates the view of the monks. " We are obedient to the Emperor in things concerning our daily life, in tribute, taxes and payments which are his due; but in ecclesiastical government we have our pastors, preachers of the word and exponents of ecclesiastical law. Political prosperity is the business of the Emperor, the ecclesiastical organisation belongs to pastors and teachers, and to take it out of their hands is to commit an act of robbery."

Here the Image-Worshippers failed to carry their point. The old theory remained, with the difference that the Emperors no longer sought to alter the Christian creed by imperial decree, for the Church as she emerged from the Iconoclast controversy had become in a fuller sense than ever the Orthodox Church; her theological development ceases. To the faith of the Fathers she has remained splendidly loyal, but that very loyalty of the heart has made it difficult for her to worship her God with all her mind. To those not of her communion who admire her unfailing devotion to her great legacy it would seem that she has lacked the courage to let the Spirit of Truth lead her into all truth, that she might be free indeed.

There remains the breach with Rome, on which a few words must be said. Through the years the gulf between East and West had widened. Even in the early fifth century communication between the Western and Eastern courts had virtually ceased unless some disagreement brought them into angry contact. In a theological age the problems of West and East were different : the interests of the Western leaders were practical and were concerned with man's relation to God—their problems were those of man's salvation or of the freedom of man's will. Under the influence of Augustine they were building up their own peculiar doctrinal system. The battles of the East were metaphysical and dealt with the mutual relations of the three Persons of the Trinity, or later with the double nature of the incarnate Son of God. In the Eastern Church an appeal to Rome was generally the last resort of a defeated minority, and the interference of the West was for the most part disciplinary, to correct the heresies of the East. For nearly half of the five centuries which lie between the accession of Constantine and the seventh œcumenical council (787) the Church of Rome was not in communion with the Church of Constantinople.

But more important still was the difference of language : while New Rome had been planted in Greek-speaking lands, in the fourth century Italy ceased to be bilingual. This astounding fact has not yet been adequately explained, but fact it remains. In the fifth century at the time of the dispute between Nestorius and Cyril of Alexandria both sides appealed to the Pope. Cyril wisely sent a Latin translation by his deacon Posidonius who knew the Western language. Until the deacon's arrival Pope Coelestin had been quite unable to answer Nestorius, as he could not read the Patriarch's letter. It would thus seem that there was no Greek scholar in Rome at the time ! In the same way the letters of the Popes to Eastern councils were first read in Latin and then translated for the understanding of the Eastern clergy, and often mistranslated, Leo the Great complains. At a council Rome was usually represented by an Eastern bishop, her own envoys being reduced to silence. Even Gregory the Great, although for years papal representative at the Court of Constantinople, could not understand Greek, and refused to answer a lady correspondent who, though a Latin, wrote to him in Greek. In the seventh century the exarch of Ravenna was driven to despair by the death of his Greek secretary. The climax was reached when a Roman Emperor in 867 spoke of Latin as a " barbarian tongue." " East and West " it has been pithily said " could come to no understanding, because quite literally they could not understand one another." Even the growth of an Eastern colony in Rome, reinforced by refugees from the Iconoclast persecution, even the journeys of Western pilgrims to the Holy Land and the restoration of Byzantine influence in Southern Italy were insufficient to bridge the gulf.

The great Byzantine patriarchs were in fact unwilling to bow to the dictation of Rome, and gladly seized an opportunity of winning popularity by an attack on the claims of the Papacy. When at the same moment patriarch and pope were men of outstanding personality schism resulted : Photius met Nicholas I (A.D. 858–867) and there was a temporary breach between Rome and Constantinople. In 1054 the masterful patriarch Cerularius disagreed with Leo IX, who was inspired with the ideals of the Cluniac reformers, and in the issue the schism became permanent. Rome had often read a lesson to Constantinople on the subject of orthodoxy : Byzantium cherished her own orthodoxy which she could defend against the West. The peculiarities of ritual which the Eastern Church had formulated in the canons of the council of 692 were championed as the Magna Charta of her ecclesiastical independence : to these Photius added the dogmatic difference on the question of the Procession of the Holy Ghost, and marshalled for all time the Byzantine case against Rome. After 1054 reunion was the bait by which the Emperors sought to secure the armed support of the West : whatever reunion may have meant to an Urban II, to the Comneni it was but a part of imperial diplomacy. When the Palæologi actually effected a temporary reconciliation with Rome, popular sentiment was outraged. To-day the Orthodox Church—the Church of the Seven Councils—still stands where she stood in the days of Photius.

It is time to take stock of the strength and weakness of the Orthodox Church. As we read its literature to-day its piety often repels us : with a living sense of the horror of sin it set supreme value on the grace of tears, and for us Western folk a fount of ready tears is an aspiration mainly confined to a

sentimental hymnody.   The generosity of
the Byzantine churchman again sprang all too
often, one feels, from the hope of repayment
in another world :

> Whatever, Lord, we lend to Thee
> Repaid a thousandfold will be;
> *Then* gladly will we give to Thee,
>   Who givest all;

is an excellent translation of East Roman
views. The East Roman Church, too, grew
to suspect humanism and sought to repress it :
the literature of the classical past was dangerous : the student of Plato was ranked with the
heretic—he was, as the " Philopatris " shows
us, regarded as a traitor. Further the Church
was a Greek Church, and it imposed the Greek
language on its worshippers, and thus
destroyed the native dialects of Asia Minor.
It had saved the Roman Empire, and later
it tended at times too completely to identify
its interest with that of the State; it asked too
little of the convert, it was too generous in
its toleration of his former faith and practice.
But there is much to be set on the other
side. It was the Greek Church which formulated for the Christian world the great
definitions of its creed; if it was in large
measure a state Church, it was yet inspired
with a missionary spirit : it sought to bring
the barbarous fringe of the Roman world
into the knowledge of the truth to which it
held with such unfailing tenacity : to it the
Slav peoples owe their conversion; it supported the state in its effort to defend oppressed

D

co-religionists: more than one war with Persia arose from succour given to Armenian Christians; admitted that it was a Greek Church, yet when it met with a *nation* it was ready to foster the vernacular language: the Syriac and Armenian literatures were created by its inspiration, and it also furnished the works which fed the new life to which it had given birth. Constantinople granted to the Slavs that liturgy in their own tongue which Rome refused to them. If it was hostile to humanism, yet it had room in its churches for the arts: practically the whole of Byzantine art that has survived is ecclesiastical art. If it at times seems subservient to the state, at others its members bear exile, torture and mutilation for the faith. If it condescended to excessive accommodation to the superstitions of its humble worshippers, it thus came very near to the people of East Rome. It lived among them, it nerved their patriotism, it became the focus of national life. In the words of Sir William Ramsay, " It moved the common, average man with more penetrating power than a loftier religion could have done. Accordingly the Orthodox Church was fitted to be the soul and life of the Empire, to maintain the Imperial unity, to give form and direction to every manifestation of national vigour." And in the dark centuries of Turkish oppression it was the Church which kept the slumbering fires of Hellenism alive, and the same Church exists to-day still loyal to its century-long endeavour.

CHAPTER VI

LAND-HOLDING AND TAXATION

Nothing is certain but death and taxes.—Benjamin
Franklin.

FOR us in twentieth-century England it is
not difficult to associate land-holding with
taxation, and for the student of the Byzantine
Empire this is no small gain, for there, if
anywhere, lawgivers and administrators
regarded the land as serving primarily the
interests of the Treasury : fiscal needs determined agricultural legislation. Taxation and
land-holding cannot well be considered apart
from each other (for Byzantine finances
generally cf. ch. vii)

Before the building up in modern times of a
great system of national and international
credit, land, immovable and indestructible,
was necessarily the safest form of investment :
capital sought land, and for similar reasons
land was sought by the state as that form of
investment which offered the greatest security
for its revenue. Thus the main pillar which
supported the whole structure of Byzantine
finance was the land tax : everywhere it was
enforced with uncompromising severity. When,

however, the new system of taxation was developed under Diocletian, the coinage of the Empire was so debased, and its value in consequence suffered such fluctuations that for the state to be paid back in its own coin meant bankruptcy; some alternative must be found for the old money tribute of fixed amount raised from the provinces. Further, it would seem difficult to escape the conclusion that in the re-fashioning of the Roman world Egypt furnished many suggestions to the statesmen of the Empire. But in Egypt imperial dues had long been paid in kind; the hungry mouths of Rome had been filled with the tribute of Egyptian corn; thus the land tax introduced by Diocletian was levied in the form of a proportion of the produce of the land. The newly-raised regiments, the hugely increased numbers of the civil service, the populace of an Eastern capital must all be fed, and the Emperors were unwilling to expend precious metal on supplies of meat and corn and oil: the provinces should provide through their taxes the rations which the sovereign was unwilling to purchase. Under Diocletian's predecessors extraordinary demands had been made on the provincials over and above their tributary obligations when large quantities of foodstuffs had been needed in case of special emergency. Now, with the fall in value of a money tribute, the extraordinary demand of the state became its ordinary revenue, but this so far kept its former character that it was not, like the money tribute, a fixed sum; it remained, as under the old conditions, an exaction determined by the needs of the moment; its amount was decided by the Emperor and his advisers. An annual estimate of the Empire's expenditure was made, and a decree—a so-called " divine delegation "—prescribed the subject's liability for the succeeding year.

But at this point we are met by the question : how was this gross liability apportioned amongst the tax-payers? Once more Egyptian conditions would seem to have suggested the answer. There where all cultivation must depend upon the Nile flood, the conditions imposed by nature upon the farmer are, so far as can be seen, unalterable. This relative permanence in Egyptian agriculture rendered it possible to divide the land into classes which were determined by the productive capacity of the soil; there was the unwatered desert, where nothing could be grown; there was ground which by an expenditure of capital on irrigation could be reclaimed for tillage; there were the rich valley tracts regularly fertilised by the Nile mud; while yet again there was land which each year lay too long under water to admit of the raising of a crop; and amongst these broad divisions there were numberless gradations in productivity. The state, recognising and registering these variations, imposed its dues upon the cultivators, their liability being determined by means of a sliding scale. This system was adopted by Diocletian for

general application to the provinces of the
Empire. Land of a certain value was taken
as the unit of taxation (iugum, later zeugarion),
broad lines of distinction were drawn in the
character of land under cultivation, and
equations thus formed. From the code of
Roman law in force in the province of Syria
we learn that a unit of 5 acres of vineyard =
20 acres of plough land = 225 olive trees (or,
if the land is hilly = 450 olive trees), while in
plough land three grades are recognised, so
that the unit may be either 20, 40 or 60 acres.
Thus the whole of the land which is capable of
production is divided into taxation units,
and these are reassessed, generally on evidence
furnished by the owners, at regular intervals.
But this tax was levied on *cultivated* land, and
it would seem that the unit of taxation
(*iugum*) was intended to be equivalent to that
amount of land which would support a single
cultivator—a *caput*. The unit could thus
be regarded from two points of view : on its
material side it represented a parcel of cultivated land, on its human side it represented
the man who tilled that parcel of land. *Jugatio*
and *Capitatio* are indeed but two aspects of
one and the same tax.[1] Obviously for the
successful application of such a system it is
essential that an equilibrium should be
maintained between these closely related
land units and work units. In a period when
population was declining the difficulty which

[1] See A. Piganiol: *L'Impôt de Capitation sous le
Bas-Empire romain.* Chambéry. 1916.

harassed alike the landed proprietor and the Roman administrator was precisely the maintenance of this equilibrium. It may well be that this constant anxiety was, at least in part, responsible for the government's determination to bind the free peasant—the *colonus*—to the soil which he cultivated.

Accordingly when the " divine delegation " had determined what was needed for the administration of the Empire in the coming year, this gross amount was divided amongst the præfectures, the prætorian præfect again made an apportionment amongst the provinces in his præfecture, the governor of the province distributed the burden amongst the municipalities of the province, the councillors of the municipalities decided the liability of the surrounding villages, and the officials of the village finally fixed the sum which fell to each unit of taxation within their district.

During the course of the fourth century there was an increasing tendency to commute renders in kind for a money payment, and ultimately this commutation was rendered general and compulsory. The assessment of the money value of the tribute was regularly fixed in the " divine delegation."

The constant aim of the sovereign was to secure, at whatever cost to his subjects, that the land should be cultivated, and that the supply of labour should not be allowed to fail. To the Roman statesman, just as much as to the legislature in medieval England, the free peasant, seeking in open market on a basis of contract to sell his labour for the highest price that it would fetch, was an economic danger. In the Roman Empire, just as in medieval England, the effect of depopulation was to raise the value of the labourer, and the Statutes of Labourers have their parallel and counterpart in the imperial constitutions of the fourth century. Just as Diocletian had sought to save the Roman world by clamping it together through the imposition of hereditary obligations, so his successors took the next step in the same direction, and bound the peasant to the soil on which he worked. Thus was established by legislative enactment the system of the colonate, for the colonus, as distinct from the slave, is a free labourer, who can acquire and hold property in his own right, but who is compelled to perform his duty as a cultivator on one and the same piece of land, or within the limits of the property of one and the same large landed proprietor. Into the many thorny questions concerning the colonate, which have given rise to a large and learned literature, we cannot enter here, but a few words as to the previous development are necessary. Here again the starting point would seem to be found in Egypt. When the Ptolemaic kings leased lands to a free peasant, it was the regular practice of the Crown to insist on a clause binding the lessee to remain on the land leased, and personally to cultivate it. Under the early Empire the African capitalists, employing free labourers on their large estates, in their turn, inserted in their agreements

like clauses probably formed on the Egyptian
model. Here we have in effect the colonate
established on a basis of *contract*. When
Marcus Aurelius and his successors settled
barbarian captives on lands within the Empire
and subjected them to a similar obligation,
it is idle any longer to say that in any real
sense the liability remained one of contract,
and in the system instituted by Diocletian of
land grants to frontier troops this obligation
has definitely passed from the sphere of contract
to that of *status*. What Diocletian had
enacted for the frontier soldiery became in the
course of the fourth century the general law
for the peasants of the Empire.

But with this principle of enforced residence
and cultivation is associated that of corporate
liability. The treasury must be secured in
any event, and the town with its surrounding
villages, represented by its council of decurions,
is thus forced to assume responsibility for the
due payment of the taxes, if in the law's
despite a tenant " flits " and leaves no one
in his place to discharge his obligations.
Since the town district bears this corporate
responsibility, it is imperative, again in the
interests of the treasury, that such a security
should exist : where it is not to be found it
must be created, and thus new councils are
called into being to shoulder the burden. How
appalling that burden was all the records of
the time show with distressing clearness, and
while wealth could by bribes secure exemption,
the poor man had nowhere to turn for help.

D 2

Only despair and flight were open to him; the liability in respect of his deserted lands descended on those who still remained, while each new bankruptcy of a decurion served but to increase the intolerable pressure which crushed the survivors. The middle classes were threatened with ruin. The village farmer sought to be protected from the claims of the state : this protection the large landholder was prepared to give—for a consideration; he became the patron—the patronus—of the village. This relation was established in many ways—perhaps the most usual was for the farmer to surrender his land into the hands of the great man, and to become his tenant. The fourth century and the first quarter of the fifth thus witnessed the struggle between the state and the large landowner. But it was not altogether obvious what was the true course for the Treasury : it wanted security for its revenue : the harassed decurions were in many cases proving a broken reed : it was clear that the big landowner could use his influence on behalf of his tenants against the state, but on the other hand if the state allowed the landowner to act as its collector of taxes, he at least was in a position through his wealth to give to the state those pledges which it sought : land, as we have already noted, was the best form of security. In 425 the latter argument gained the day, and the state capitulated to the patronus, and thus vast tracts of the country-side were withdrawn from that communal responsibility for the taxes which had rested on the decurions, while in the course of the fifth century the village community became immediately responsible for its quota of taxation. The fifth and sixth centuries are thus marked by the growth in the power of the great landed proprietors, and from one point of view the subsequent history of the Empire is a struggle between the state and the landed aristocracy. For, apart from the purely financial question, it is obvious that it was in the interest of the central government to encourage the small farmer, and to reduce the dangerous authority of the feudal lord. The sixth century saw private citizens forming armed bands of retainers— Buccellarii—and this military force was a standing menace to the peace of the provinces : fishing in troubled waters was a profitable occupation, and in the pages of John of Nikiu we are given a vivid picture of the distraction which the feuds of these great nobles could cause : with their train-bands they were able to set the civil authorities at defiance. But their power was largely broken in the seventh century by the inroads on the North of Slav and Avar hordes, and by the invasion of the east and south, first by Persian, and then by Arab armies. When order had once more been restored by the Heraclian house, there was a new chance for the small proprietor. But in the tenth century the aristocratic landlords of Asia Minor so strengthened their position that in the eleventh century they could lay violent hands upon the central government itself.

But it is time we looked somewhat more closely at the life of the villages in the Byzantine Empire as pictured for us in the Farmer's Law. And first we must distinguish between the free village and the servile village. The peasants in both are equally chained to the land which they cultivate, but while in the servile village the land is the lord's, and it is he who is responsible to the state for all taxation on behalf of his slaves who have no absolute right to any property which they may acquire (it can always be claimed by their master), in the free village—that inhabited by the coloni—the land belongs to the village community, or to the farmers themselves, and the latter are free to acquire and dispose of property. If we entered a free village under the Byzantine Empire we should find that the land consists of vineyards and garden patches where vegetables are grown, of the plough lands, and of pasture. The vineyards and gardens are enclosed with a ditch and fence of sharp stakes, on which the cattle at times impale themselves. The plough lands are unenclosed, but for the most part they are held in full private ownership, and within the limits of the village community the farmer can dispose of them as he will. As for the pasture lands we must not think of them as meadows, which, like our English fields, can be used now as arable land, and now as grazing ground. The pastures are those lands which are not capable of cultivation—uncleared woodland or rough scrub. They lie on the outer ring, furthest removed from the centre of village life. They probably belong in the main to the community, and then as bit by bit they are occupied by one peasant and another, a clearing is made, they are brought under cultivation, and then a " division " or partition takes place and another piece of land passes into private ownership. But the woodland too may be in private ownership, and then if any other farmer should enter with the owner's consent and reclaim it, for three years he can keep the profit for himself, but at the end of that time the owner can reassert his rights : but if the farmer enters and sows without the owner's consent, he cannot claim his crop. On these common woodlands the cattle are taken out to graze in the morning by the neatherds with their strong fierce dogs, and in the evening they are driven back to the pen. Each sheep or ox carries a bell round its neck, for it may easily stray : and if a thief cuts off the bell and the beast is lost, the thief must make good the loss. The chief property of the village community probably lies in its herds and flocks, and the herdsman receives a wage for his work. The small proprietor entrusts his own ox or sheep to the herdsman, and the latter takes it out to graze with the village herd : if it strays and does damage to the tilth or vineyards, the herdsman will, it is true, not lose his wage, but he must make good the damage. Outside the village there are wild beasts : the wolves are always ready to devour the sheep or asses :

at times they break into the fold at night, and then woe to the thief who has stolen the sheep dog, for he must make good the whole flock of sheep as well as the value of the dog. After harvest the cattle are allowed to graze on the stubble, but no man may let his beasts into his own ground until all his neighbours have got in their crops. The daily life of the peasant community can indeed be illustrated in a wealth of detail from our sources, but here we have only space to notice a few further points. First as to the position of the farmer : he may be owner of his own plot of land, and, if so, within the limits of the community he has complete power of disposition. He may be a tenant, and, if so, he may be either a tenant of a farm which is already in good cultivation, or he may be a tenant to whom uncultivated land is leased with the obligation of reclaiming it. In the former case the farm buildings will already be erected, and the landlord will provide the necessary capital. The farm will be leased for a short period only, perhaps on a yearly tenancy, and the tenant pays the landlord what corresponds to a rack rent—half the yearly produce. In the latter case, the tenant must provide the capital and in fact create a farm : his tenancy is consequently either perpetual or for a long term of years : he pays a customary rent of one-tenth of the produce, and is probably under further obligations to render services and contributions in kind to his landlord. In the case, however, of the farmer proprietor his right freely to dispose of his land was subject to one important limitation.

Within this village community the ties of family are naturally strong, and when two farmers are joint proprietors, they are almost certainly related to each other, and thus when one of them wishes to sell his undivided share of the land, his relative has a right of pre-emption, if he will pay the price that the stranger offers; and even if the joint owners are not relatives, but only partners, they enjoy a similar right.

Later this principle was based on a new foundation, and more widely applied. The village community is, as we have seen, cor-porately liable to the state for its taxes : when any land within the community falls out of cultivation, as, for instance, through the flight of its owner, the state to safeguard its revenue can compel a solvent proprietor to undertake the cultivation of such land, and to render himself liable for the taxes in respect of it—provided that such additional land is of moderate extent when compared with the proprietor's original holding. As a result of this every member of the community was concerned in the solvency of every other, and thus the right of pre-emption was ultimately enjoyed by every member of the village. The right rested no longer on the ground of kinship, or association, but merely on that of a common financial interest.

But the free farmer's right of disposition was not without its dangers, for the large landed proprietor was always anxious to increase his holding, and it was easy to compel the humble free owner to part with his land in favour of his powerful neighbour. The reforming legislation of the tenth century endeavoured to impose an absolute prohibition upon the acquisition by the large landed proprietor of any land within the village community, whether such acquisition were by way of gift, or for a valuable consideration, and whether such large proprietor were a lay lord, or an ecclesiastical house. Indeed in the laws of the tenth century the Mortmain Acts of Medieval England, though passed with a different aim, find their counterpart. But in this form the prohibition could not be maintained, and later legislation adopted the rule that alienations of land could only be effectively made between parties of the same social standing—the poor can convey to the poor, the rich to the rich, but in every case to those of their own rank alone. The legal principle of free alienation has given way before the political necessity of safeguarding the defenceless : similar developments in our own time (*e.g.* the Workmen's Compensation Acts, the Trade Disputes Act) are not far to seek : for the power of the limited company and the large employer of labour stands to the workman of to-day much in the same position of economic superiority as the great landed proprietor to the small farmer of the East Roman Empire, and then, as now, it was realised that a people's safety is the supreme law before which legal theories must give place. But from another point of view this tenth-century legislation is not without its interest, for it resulted in a still more sweeping recognition of that hierarchic classification of society which lies at the heart of the fourth-century reconstruction. It may be regarded as the final triumph of the principle of status over that of contract.

CHAPTER VII

THE CIVIL ADMINISTRATION

The vices of authority are chiefly four : delays,
corruption, roughness and facility.—BACON, *Of
Great Place.*

I. *The Bureaucracy*

HE who would treat of the bureaucratic
system of East Rome must either write very
much or very little, for the subject is one of
extreme complexity. Discretion and a regard
for the reader are conclusive : we follow the
latter course.

The fundamental administrative principle
of the reorganisation of Diocletian and
Constantine was the complete separation of
the duties of the military commander (*dux*)
and the civil governor (*praeses*); and this
was combined with a general reduction in
the size of the provinces : neither commander
nor governor was to enjoy an authority which
might make him a dangerous rival to the
throne. Power must be centralised in the
hands of the Emperor and with this end in
view an elaborate hierarchy was constituted.
All jurisdiction flowed from the sovereign, and
that jurisdiction was itself controlled through

the subject's ultimate recourse to the sovereign by way of appeal. The Emperor was alike source of law and of authority, and interpreter of that law and of the limits of that delegated authority. In the developed administrative system, as we see it, for instance, under Theodosius I towards the close of the fourth century, the empire is divided into four præfectures; at the head of each is a prætorian præfect; each præfecture is in turn divided into a varying number of dioceses under *vicarii*, each of such dioceses being composed of a complex of provinces ruled by governors; the governor is in general subject to the vicarius, the vicarius is subordinated to the præfect, and the præfect to the Emperor. For the præfect has now become part of the civil hierarchy, and thus the long process which through the second and third centuries had tended to give to the office an increasingly civil and judicial character reaches its consummation. His sole concern with matters military now arises from his duty to enforce the conscription of recruits and to superintend the supply of the Army's rations; he would thus naturally be consulted with regard to the movements of troops within his præfecture. To him the Emperor addresses the laws which are to be enforced throughout the provinces which he administers, and he himself has the power of issuing edicts provided that they do not conflict with the laws. He determines the amount of the taxes to be raised in any year, though any increase or remission of such taxation requires the Emperor's approval. His control over the provincial governors he exercises mainly through his vicarii, but it is important to realise that the vicarius within his diocese is not merely the agent of the præfect; he is appointed by the Emperor and can report to him directly. Thus an elaborate system of check and counter-check was constituted, for while it was always open to the Emperor to send special commissioners to inspect the local administration, and while he could at any time communicate immediately and not necessarily through the intervention of the præfect with the vicar of the diocese or the governor of the province, each of these officials jealously watched the proceedings of the other; further the governor was no longer the sole authority within the province; by his side stood the military commander, exercising a power co-ordinate with and independent of the governor.

In the capital itself the principal minister was the Master of the Offices. Under his control were the Palace Guards and also the great arsenals of the Empire. All communications from the provincial administrators passed through his hands, and he was at the head of the four great bureaux which conducted the imperial correspondence. Since he introduced all ambassadors from other states, he was able to exercise much influence on foreign policy, while he also supervised the postal system through which the Court kept in touch with its governors. His office continually gained in power at the expense of the Prætorian Præfecture.

The two great finance ministers were the Count of the Sacred Largesses and the Count of the Private Estates. The former was not merely, as his name might suggest, the High Almoner of the Emperor, for by this time the Privy Purse had really become the State Treasury, and the Count of the Sacred Largesses was now responsible for the general finances of the Empire. The Count of the Private Estates managed the wide imperial domains which had been swelled by the successive confiscations of former sovereigns. The Prætorian Præfects had also their own treasuries out of which they provided for the needs of the Army.

The internal administration of the capital was in the hands of the Præfect of the City, while it was policed by the train-bands of the Circus parties—the demesmen.

The division of the provinces into smaller units and the constitution of the new hierarchy of officials created the need for a vast imperial service with ordered and regular promotion. By the side of the hierarchy of office a hierarchy of rank with high-sounding titles was developed. The separation of the civil and military careers tended towards concentration and greater efficiency, and at the same time gave rise to a rigid administrative tradition. The strength of this intensely conservative force acted as a corrective

to hasty innovation : an Emperor might
enjoin changed methods and altered principles
of government, but he was mortal and his
days were short : the life of the bureaucratic
machine was long; men quietly reverted to
the old paths. The freaks of a despot were
powerless against the massive stability of the
whole body of the state's servants, but on
the other hand this same dead weight of
tradition broke many a reformer's heart and
will. To read the edicts of Justinian is to
see laid bare the tragedy of an Emperor's
good intentions.

Under the strain of the attacks upon the
Empire which fill the history of the seventh
century this divine hierarchy of office broke
down, and, in the gradual reconstruction
which followed, co-ordination of officials took
the place of the former subordination. The
hierarchy of rank remains and is yet further
elaborated, but the hierarchy of office is no
more. The provinces become military districts and the general is the governor (see
ch. vii), but he takes his orders from the
Emperor alone : the Masters of Soldiers and
the Prætorian Præfects disappear, and as a
result the office of Præfect of the City gains
in importance. The great central ministries
of the Master of the Offices, the Count of the
Sacred Largesses and the Count of the Sacred
Estate each with many subordinate depart-
ments were broken up into a large number of
co-ordinate offices with restricted competence,
while on the other hand there comes into

existence one central minister of finance, the *Sacellarius*, who in the ninth century exercised a general and methodical control over all the offices which dealt with finance or administered the sources of revenue; the disadvantage of not possessing a single central exchequer was thus to a certain extent mitigated.

Though in later years some offices might decline in authority (*e.g.* that of the City Præfect), and though new offices might be created, yet the broad lines of this reconstruction seem to have been preserved until the fall of Constantinople in 1204 : indeed from one point of view the history of the twelfth century consists of a struggle for power between the civil servant and the military aristocracy of Asia Minor. Despite financial difficulty and in the face of many perils the administrative tradition never died.

Immensely costly, often corrupt, slow to move and unrelenting when set in motion, the bureaucracy of East Rome was yet an effective and scientifically organised engine of government : it rendered possible the existence of that social life based upon the rule of law which distinguished the Empire from the lands which lay beyond its frontiers.

II. *Administration of Justice*

It is thus natural that we should consider briefly the administration of justice in this East Roman world. The sovereign, we have seen, is the final interpreter of the law which he promulgates. From the judgments of all courts an appeal lies to the Emperor, save when, in the earlier period, the case came before the court of the Prætorian Præfect acting as the Emperor's delegate; here the Præfect's judgment was final. The subject, if he deems himself wronged, can state his complaint through the Ministry of Petitions, and on failing to obtain redress, he may even seek justice of the Emperor in person. Thus Theophilus regularly heard suitors in his weekly procession through the capital to the church of the Virgin in Blachernae. After the abolition of the office of the prætorian præfect, at the head of the administration of justice in the capital itself was the City Præfect, assisted by the quæstor, though from the middle of the eleventh century the præfect's jurisdiction was exercised by the Great Drungar. In Constantinople, too, sat a High Court composed of twelve judges to whose decision the Emperor could remit important questions of law, while for cases of less moment there were inferior courts of which we know but little. Outside the capital the provincial judges administered justice, their judgments, of course, being subject to appeal. In civil matters the ecclesiastical courts had jurisdiction where the defendant was an ecclesiastic, while the parties could by mutual consent give the ecclesiastical courts jurisdiction in any civil suit. In the eleventh century questions relating to marriage or to pious foundations made for the benefit of the grantee's soul were directed by Alexius Comnenus to be tried by the Church Courts (A.D. 1086); and these courts in general decided all civil cases where both plaintiff and defendant were ecclesiastics. During the last centuries of the restored Empire the sharp line of distinction between Church and civil courts was obscured, and this growing influence of the clergy in the administration of justice became only more prominent after the Turkish conquest.

The most remarkable feature of Byzantine criminal law is the frequency with which mutilation was employed as a punishment. This practice, which may have taken its rise in customary procedure, was adopted as a general principle by the Iconoclast Emperors, and though it may be argued that in some instances mutilation was inflicted where under Justinian the death penalty had previously been exacted, and that in fact capital punishment tended to disappear, yet it must be confessed that this plea has no application in many cases where later criminal law subjected the offender to blinding, nose-slitting or to the loss of hand or tongue. This fatal heritage received a further development at the hands of the Turks after the fall of Constantinople. It is true that the harshness of the legislator was to some extent modified by the right of asylum—the right of the clergy to afford shelter to the accused so long as he remained within the precincts of the church—but to many classes of offenders this refuge was denied.. Beside mutilation, confiscation of property was a frequent form of punishment, but not so imprisonment, which, at least until the twelfth century, was only employed to prevent the escape of the criminal before trial.[1] Zachariae von Lingenthal long ago remarked that for the Byzantine *far niente* was a delight, and no hardship.

Successive emperors strove earnestly to make it easy for their subjects to assert their rights; an effort was even made to support country suitors out of public funds during their stay in the capital pending the hearing of their case; but the student of Byzantine history must fear that all too often litigants, remembering that Justice was blindfold, slipped the weight of surreptitious gold into her scales.

III. *Finance*

Nowhere more acutely than in the sphere of finance does the historian of the East Roman Empire feel the limitations which the silence of his sources imposes upon him. He would gladly sacrifice the details of some frontier war recorded by a chronicler, if he could only obtain in exchange some further insight into the working of that system which alone enabled the Emperors to main-

---

[1] Enforced seclusion in a monastery was, however, occasionally practised in the case of state offenders.

tain and equip their armies. But it must be
regretfully admitted that we cannot reconstruct the Byzantine budget : we can only
in a general way consider the main items of
expenditure, the principal sources of income.

The first charge upon the state was the
cost of its defence—the cost of army and of
fleet, of frontier fortresses and harbours, of
munitions of war and mercenary soldiers;
and many an Emperor discovered, as did
Justinian, that his schemes of military
expansion were impracticable, because they
outran the resources of the Empire. Then
the expenses of the Court, though exceed-
ingly heavy, could not with safety be curtailed,
for, as we have seen, court ceremony was in
Byzantine state theory something more than
idle display, it was an important element in
imperial diplomacy : it was justified by a
conception of sovereignty which was funda-
mentally religious : the earthly empire must
mirror the splendours of the heavenly, and,
thus festivals, both secular and ecclesiastical,
processions, receptions, and the voyages and
journeyings of the Court made inexorable
demands upon the treasury. Further, on
occasions such as these custom prescribed
that gifts should be made to high officials
and to the bishops and clergy, while the poor
of the capital also shared in the imperial
largess. When a province was visited by
some special calamity, as by an earthquake,
the sovereign's generosity would come to the
relief of the sufferers; the state contributed

towards the reconstruction of ruined cities, or it might be necessary for some years to accord a remission of taxation.

The public buildings raised by the Emperors absorbed vast sums, while in the early centuries there was also the heavy expenditure necessitated by the public distribution to the inhabitants of Constantinople of bread, meat, wine, and oil. The financial crisis in the first decade of the reign of Heraclius forced the Emperor to suspend this distribution, and there is apparently no evidence for its subsequent renewal. Grain was still stored by the state in public granaries, but it would seem that this was rather in order to meet the demands of the army.

But throughout the Empire public works had to be maintained—aqueducts, cisterns, roads and bridges—while a special tax was levied for the repair of the walls of the capital; inscriptions still testify to the constant care with which successive Emperors guarded these essential defences.

Finally the claims of religion must not be forgotten. Under this head falls the support of orphanages, of hospitals, of retreats for aged folk who could no longer earn their own living, as well as of maternity homes and houses of refuge for fallen women. The Emperors were themselves Byzantines, and felt as strongly as their subjects the attractions of monastic piety and the need to make provision for their souls; thus ecclesiastical foundations often absorbed large sums, while if these gifts, as was usual, were accompanied by grants of imperial lands, the income of the state would suffer from the immunities from taxation conferred upon the monastery or the institution to which the endowment was conveyed.

Any attempt to estimate the annual revenue of the Byzantine state must remain purely hypothetical. We possess only two statements upon which to base a conjecture. Benjamin of Tudela writes that in the twelfth century from Constantinople alone the treasury drew 7,300,000 nomismata, while in 1205 the Crusaders promised Baldwin the Latin ruler of Constantinople a daily income of 30,000 nomismata (a nomisma = 12s.). To these may be added John Brompton's assertion that in 1190 Corfu paid 1500 gold litrai (= £64,800 worth of metal, not purchasing power) to the state. From these inadequate data it is idle to attempt to estimate the annual income of the East Roman Empire.

What were the sources of revenue from which the state met its liabilities? These were mainly (i) property of the subject lapsing to the Treasury (on account of the death of the owner intestate, and without leaving children or relatives), (ii) direct gifts by subjects, (iii) the payments made by candidates for office at court or in the civil service, (iv) the income of the imperial domains in Asia, and finally (v) taxation direct and indirect, ordinary and extraordinary.

As to the first there is in Byzantine law no distinction for the purpose of intestate succession between realty and personalty, and on the failure of all those entitled to participate in the distribution, the whole property of the deceased passed as *bona vacantia* to the state : a modification was introduced by Constantine Porphyrogenitus in the tenth century, and henceforth in such cases one-third passed to the Church for the benefit of the soul of the deceased, and two-thirds only to the treasury.   As regards the third source of income it was the general practice of the later Empire to demand from a candidate for office a sum of money on which his salary may be regarded as an annual payment in the nature of interest. On election the official, it is true, could increase his income by the receipt of customary fees and presents and other less legitimate means, but as a rule his salary itself represented but a modest return on his capital, rarely more than 3 per cent.[1]   But it was principally to taxation that the state looked for its revenue, and here the land tax was always the key-stone of Byzantine finance. This we have already considered so far as it affected agricultural land, but the so-called *aerikon*, introduced in the reign of Justinian, was perhaps a similar tax imposed on land

---

[1] These offices were, however, frequently only court sinecures, entitling the holder to a place in a hierarchy of rank ; cf. A. Andréadès in *Nouvelle Revue historique de droit français*, XLV. (1921).

which was covered by buildings. It would
thus be the urban parallel to the rural land-
tax. It is possible that the hearth-tax of
the time of the Comneni was the successor
of the *aerikon* of the sixth century. The tax
of 5 per cent. on inheritances, though abolished
by Justinian, was, it would seem, subsequently
revived. The legislation of the fourth century
had freed senators from municipal taxes, but
they were liable to a special property tax (the
gleba) and were also subjected to an irregular
tax—the *aurum oblaticium*—a payment made
to the Emperor on anniversaries of his accession or on occasion of a victory. Finally
until the reign of Anastasius a tax was levied
on the earnings of all those carrying on any
trade, whether it were that of huckster,
cobbler, baker or prostitute it mattered not;
if city dwellers brought their wares or their
bodies for sale, they were liable to this tax,
which though nominally exacted every five
years on the celebration by the Emperor of
his Quinquennalia, was as a matter of fact
collected much more frequently. Peasants,
however, bringing their own agricultural
produce to market were at an early date
accorded exemption. Though this hated imposition was abolished by Anastasius, a
similar tax appears shortly after to have
taken its place; the Empress Irene won
popularity by its suppression.

Apart from direct taxation the state drew
a large income from customs levied at such
stations as Jotabe (on Eastern merchandise

coming up the Arabian Gulf) or Abydos, while it was sought to render illicit trading more difficult by offering commissions to informers. These duties were a legacy from the earlier Empire, and a constitution of the Antonine period enables us to draw up a list of the most important articles subject to taxation. Among them may be mentioned spices, cotton-stuffs, costly skins from Babylon or Persia, ivory, precious stones, dyes and eastern wools. Eastern slaves, pages and eunuchs were also subject to customs duties.

The Treasury further increased its revenue by the exaction of harbour dues and market tolls, and by the profits from state monopolies such as the manufacture of silk. The sovereign could also demand from his subjects forced services (*angareia*) such as maintenance of stations and the supply of horses for the imperial post, as well as the entertainment of ambassadors or other officials on their journeys through the provinces. As a final source of income may be mentioned fines imposed by the law courts, while the punishment of confiscation of a subject's property often offered a tempting means of escape from financial embarrassments.

As we study the system of Byzantine finance we note an increasing tendency to substitute money payments for renders in kind, and this gold wealth of the East Roman Emperor has a significance which has not always been fully recognised. In the German

states of the West there was no direct land-
tax; the King for the support of his court
was forced to look to the revenues drawn from
his own royal lands : payment to the officers
of the Crown was thus made not in money,
but in land grants, and the holders of such
lands were not subject to direct taxation
which could be regulated to meet the current
needs of the state, but were only bound to
render fixed services under conditions which
were themselves strictly defined. But payment in land grants carried with it a permanent relation of the grantee to the land
granted, with the natural result that the
rights which he had exercised over the land
tended to become hereditary; and since land
capital cannot be increased at will the king
became progressively impoverished : to aug-
ment his wealth he must either confiscate
the fief of his vassal, or enlarge his frontiers.
Herein lies the explanation of much of the
aggression of western rulers in the early
middle ages, especially in their schemes of
Italian conquest : but in the conquered
territory the same process repeated itself,
and through the weakness of the central power
the vassal soon ceased to be a support to
his sovereign : he identified himself with local
interests, and imperial authority had to be
reasserted by military intervention. Thus
a western power can maintain neither standing army, nor fleet : its forces are raised for
a campaign, not for the course of a war : its
action is spasmodic.

E

When we turn to the Eastern Empire, the difference is obvious : here generals are paid from time to time in coin, and not in permanent land grants; the central power maintains its control. Further money-capital is capable of increase, because the land-holders remain subject to taxation, the amount of which is not fixed once and for all : thus increase of the Crown's wealth does not carry with it the necessity for internal dislocation, or foreign conquest. Thereby a standing army and an imperial fleet in being become possibilities : a long service army can be trained and scientifically organised : military pressure on an enemy is sustained, and not subject to constant intermission. In a word the action of the state is continuous and not merely spasmodic : and herein lies the secret of the success of East Rome. Individual Emperors might be spend-thrifts, but the financial machine remained, and in the succeeding reign recuperation followed. The wonder of Byzantine finance is indeed its permanency, resting in large measure on the purity of its gold coinage. " In the period of 800 years," writes Gelzer, " from Diocletian to Alexius Comnenus the Roman government never found itself compelled to declare bankruptcy, or stop payments. Neither the ancient nor the modern world can offer a complete parallel to this phenomenon. This prodigious stability of Roman financial policy secured the " byzant " its universal currency. On account of its

full weight it passed with all the neighbouring nations as a valid medium of
exchange. By her money Byzantium controlled both the civilised and the barbarian
worlds."

CHAPTER VIII

THE ARMY AND NAVY

Above all, for Empire and greatness, it importeth most that a nation do profess arms as their principal honour, study, and occupation.—BACON, *Of Kingdoms*.

I. *The Army*

THE history of Rome is the history of the Roman army, and in nothing is Byzantium more truly the heir of Rome than in her military policy. The empire had been won and safeguarded by the legions, and the strength of the legion lay in its infantry. The outstanding feature in the later history of Rome's army is the gradual growth of the supremacy of the cavalry : the few remaining infantry regiments occupied but a subordinate position. Originally to the legion recruited from Roman citizens was attached a small body of horse raised from Rome's allies (the *auxilia*) : it was probably the foresight of the brilliant but unfortunate Gallienus that divined the need for mobile troops of cavalry formed as separate units independent of the legions. The wonder of the fourth century writers is the new force of cavalry clothed in chain-mail after the Persian model (the *cata-*

phracti): the first great cavalry battle is the
tremendous struggle between Constantius and
the rival Emperor Magnentius (Battle of
Mursa), and in the wars with Persia in the
fourth century the importance of the cavalry
is everywhere manifest from the pages of
Ammianus Marcellinus. The lesson was only
accentuated by Rome's defeat at Adrianople
in 378, where the success of the Goths was
due to a brilliant cavalry charge. In the
account which Procopius gives of Justinian's
wars we often read that a force was composed
only of horsemen, and the supremacy of the
cavalry was finally assured by the reorganisation of the army under the house of Heraclius
and the military reforms of the Isaurian
Emperors. The victories of the Macedonian
sovereigns were won in the main by mounted
troops.

The history of the organisation of the
Roman army must be very briefly traced.
The system introduced by Diocletian and
Constantine was, as we know, based upon a
complete severance of civil and military
authority : its aim was to provide for the
defence of the frontiers, and behind this
frontier guard to create a mobile force which
could be moved to the support of any province
threatened by invasion. The Prætorian guard
was abolished, and a new guard—the *Comitatenses*, those attached to the comitatus—
the suite of the Emperor—formed. The bad
old days of the Prætorian king-makers were
to be a thing of the past. The frontier force

—the *limitanei*—were given inalienable grants
of land, and the son was under a hereditary
obligation to step into his father's place.
The Comitatenses and the regiments subsequently raised, the curiously named *Pseudo-
Comitatenses*, became the regular imperial
army, and new court troops, the *Protectores*
and *Domestici*, in their turn took their place
as a palace guard. The frontier force in
each province was commanded by a *dux*
(general), the imperial army was under
magistri—masters of foot or horse : later
both infantry and cavalry were united under
the single command of a master of foot or
horse, or of a master of both services. This
system remained substantially unaltered under
Justinian, though since the creation of the
regiments of federate Goths by Theodosius
the Great the number of barbarians serving
in separate troops under their own officers
had grown greatly, while the barbarian element
in the regular army had steadily increased.
The most dangerous innovation, however,
was the introduction of a system similar to
the Western usage whereby men undertook
service under a particular general, and looked
to him rather than to the state for their
support. The soldiers " who served for their
rations " (*Buccellarii :* buccellum = the military biscuit) obviously tended to relax the
discipline of the regular army, and the pages
of Procopius are full of examples of the
insubordination of Roman troops—a lack of
discipline which was often not without excuse,

for the men's pay was constantly in arrear
and their equipment scandalously insufficient.
But of the Roman horse-archer of his day
Procopius speaks with pardonable pride.

In several cases Justinian broke through
the fundamental principle of the reforms of
Diocletian and Constantine by uniting in
one hand both civil and military authority :
Maurice's measures pointed in the same
direction : by the creation of the position of
exarch—supreme military commander—in
Italy and Africa the civil governor was subordinated to the general. The seventh century
was, as we have already seen, a period of
continuous wars, and under the Heraclian
dynasty a new division of the Empire into
"themes" was gradually evolved. The
history of this development is hidden from
us through our lack of material, but the
system was based upon military needs; the
military commander had precedence over the
civil governor, and the importance of the
themes of Asia Minor during the time when
the new organisation was being formed is
reflected in the fact that the officers of the
Eastern themes always enjoyed precedence
at Court and also drew higher pay. The
Isaurian sovereigns completed this reorganisation of the Empire, and now both civil and
military power were vested in the military
commander; Rome had thus reverted once
more to the position under the Republic :
then the civil governor was also general,
when the need arose; now the general was

also civil governor. To quote Professor Bury, who has made notable contributions towards the elucidation of the details of Byzantine military organisation, " The *strategos* (general) of a large theme commanded a corps of 10,000, and the scheme of the divisions and subordinate commands has a remarkable resemblance to the organisation of some of the armies of modern Europe. The recorded scheme was probably not uniform in all the themes, and varied at different periods. The *Thema* (army-corps) consisted of two *turmai* (brigades) under *turmarchai*—the turma of five *banda* (regiments) each under a *drungarios* (colonel), the bandon of five *pentarkhiai* under a *kometes* (captain). The pentarkhia containing 200 men had five subdivisions under *pentekontarchai* (lieutenants) and there was a smaller unit of 10 men under the *dekarkhes* (corporal). The total strength in the ninth century was 120,000, in Justinian's time it was reckoned at 150,000." If one considers these figures in the light of the armies kept on foot by the modern states who at the present day rule over the lands once subject to the Roman Empire, the achievements of the small Byzantine forces will be more truly appreciated.

The cost of the upkeep of these provincial troops was charged upon the inhabitants of the different themes, and was raised in the eastern themes by payments in money made to the central treasury, in the western by renders in kind. It has been suggested that this difference is due to the fact that in the west the inhabitants were very largely Slav farmers engaged in agriculture, while the city with its money economy was for the most part confined to the Greek districts on the coast. When in the twelfth century the central government endeavoured to introduce into the west the money economy of the eastern provinces, Bulgaria revolted, and the second Bulgarian Empire arose.

Our information with regard to the provincial militia is insufficient for any adequate account of its value or organisation.

But beyond the armies of the themes in the ninth century we are able to trace the organisation of the city troops—the *tagmata* —garrisoned in the capital, with detachments stationed in Thrace and Macedonia. These regiments of palace guards had been entirely reorganised since the time of Justinian and their numbers reduced. Each regiment was as a rule under the command of a Domesticus, and one of these, the Domesticus of the Scholae, who had taken the place of the Master of the Offices, became in the tenth century the commander in chief of the whole army. These palace troops only went on active service when the Emperor took the field in person. The infantry regiment of the Numeri, also stationed in the capital, and the forces under the Domesticus of the Walls (? = the Long walls of Anastasius) were comparatively unimportant.

The outstanding difference between the

E 2

armies of Justinian and those raised after the close of the sixth century lies in the fact that the foreign mercenaries tend to disappear; the army is raised from within the Empire, more especially from Armenia, though the great Hetæriarch still commands a corps of guards—largely foreigners—representing in all probability the *Foederati* (*i. e.* barbarian troops supplied under the terms of a treaty) of an earlier date.

The system of grants of land on condition of military service, which had in the fourth century been employed in the case of the frontier guard, was revived and extended throughout the themes. These grants were similarly inalienable, and entailed a hereditary obligation to serve in the army of the province.

But the military system which had been developed under the brilliant soldier sovrans of the Macedonian house never recovered from the crushing victory of the Seljuks at the battle of Manzikert (1071), when the Emperor Romanus was taken prisoner.

The decline of the East Roman army in the eleventh and twelfth centuries was indeed mainly due to two causes: in Asia Minor the Seljuk conquests won much territory from the Empire, and worse still, since the Seljuks were mere barbarians with a lust for plunder and destruction, even in the territories which remained Roman, the land ran to waste under their forays, while the peasants were forced to flee from their farms and take refuge in the cities. At the same time the

growth of a powerful military nobility, whose
influence was founded upon the possession
of large estates in Asia Minor, caused grave
anxiety to the central government. While
the civil administration sought to weaken
this dangerous spirit of aristocratic independence by the imposition of heavy taxation, the state, no longer strong enough for a
direct attack upon the privileges of the great
landlords, endeavoured to create a counter-
poise by extensive territorial grants to soldiers.
Of this new system of *pronia* (= provision)
introduced by Michael VII Ducas and developed under the Comneni we are unfortunately imperfectly informed. Apparently, like
the early fiefs of Western Europe, the grant
was made for the lifetime of the donee only
—all rights of inheritance were excluded.
The grant, which was, it seems, coupled with
an obligation of residence upon the land, was
only made to soldiers of high rank, and in
general as a reward for past services. The
grantee was bound to supply a certain number
of recruits to the army. In return for this
the state surrendered to him its right to
raise certain taxes within his *pronia*, though
any arbitrary increase of the tenants' burdens
was forbidden : he was also given certain
privileges with regard to the administration
of justice and the maintenance of police.
These lands were not, it appears, taken from
the estates of the nobility, nor from the
domains of the church, but the land-hunger
of the aristocracy would often lead to the

incorporation in their estates of these military holdings and to the consequent weakening of the efficiency of the army.

The twelfth-century Emperors were further faced by a very serious decline in the free population of the Empire. The ravages of the Seljuks in Asia were paralleled by those of Hungarians and Serbs in Europe. The Comneni sought by all means in their power to make good these losses. Turks and Patzinaks were settled as colonists within the Empire, slaves were liberated at the public cost, while the campaigns against the Hungarians became man hunts on a large scale. As a result of this depopulation the armies of the Empire were once more composed of mercenaries, of foreign vassals and allies, among them Lombards, Franks, Germans, Serbs, and even the troops of Mohammedan Emirs, while the Imperial guard consisted for the most part of English soldiers. It is this change of military policy which proved fatal under the Angeli, when the impoverished state failed to pay its mercenaries. *Point d'argent, point de Suisse.*

We are fortunate in possessing several military handbooks dating from various periods in the history of the East Roman Empire. It is only from a study of these that one can really understand the greatness of this Byzantine army. Here alone in the Europe of the middle ages was the business of war treated with scientific elaboration, each generation facing new problems, and solving them by close and sustained study. Here it was not numbers, but reasoned skill which carried the day; a battle was no disordered mêlée, but the disciplined co-operation of many units. Byzantine generals could not afford to indulge in a passion for quixotic chivalry: too much depended on the preservation of their small forces. Thus it was the commander's duty to secure conditions favourable to the Roman arms before venturing on an engagement. Feigned flight, night attacks, ambushes, negotiations only intended to win time—whatever the means, all was fair in war, and the soldier who relied on force where subtlety could win the day was a fool for his pains. Training, bravery, discipline and a pride in their profession— these are the characteristics of the Byzantine soldier, as they are seen for instance in the book of instruction which Kekaumenos wrote for his son; and as his commander never failed to remind him, every campaign was a crusade, in which the victory was God-given; but, while this was true, to gain that gift man must play his part. Only so long as the Roman military tradition is maintained will Heaven grant success to the forces of Rome.

Both cavalry and infantry were divided into heavy and light-armed horse and foot. The heavy-armed trooper wore a steel cap, a long mail shirt reaching from the neck to the thighs, gauntlets and steel shoes. He carried a light cloak or burnous to wear over his armour in the heat of summer, and a

large woollen cloak as shelter against cold
or wet. His arms were a broad sword, a
dagger, a long lance and a horseman's bow
and quiver, while, if he were riding in the
front rank, his charger would be protected
by steel poitrails and frontlets.

The light armed horseman was usually an
archer, wearing a coat of mail. The heavy
armed foot-soldier also wore a mail-shirt and
steel helmet : his weapons were the sword,
the lance, and the axe with a cutting blade
at one side and a spike at the other. The
light armed foot-soldier was either an archer
or a javelin-man. He wore a tunic reaching
to the knees and at times a light mail-shirt.
He carried a quiver with forty arrows, and an
axe at his belt : slung at his back was a
small round buckler.

This Byzantine army possessed an extraordinarily effective organisation. It had its
own R.A.M.C. : the mounted *deputati* of the
medical service carried the wounded from
the field of battle back to military doctors.
Its engineers had studied in detail all the
natural difficulties which would have to be
surmounted in a campaign. To take but one
example : for the passage of broad rivers,
where a western army would have been
forced to march until a ford was reached, the
Byzantines constructed sectional boats, of
which the numbered parts could be borne
on the backs of the transport animals, and
then put together rapidly and caulked when
the stream was reached. Castramenation was

still a living science, and as late as the tenth century had a special literature of its own, while the Armenians and the aristocratic families of Asia Minor produced a long succession of brilliant generals.

To read a Byzantine military text-book with its detailed instructions as to the method by which the various enemies of the Empire may be met and conquered is to gain a splendid panoramic view of the ethnography of Europe in the early middle ages. The military forces of the Empire formed in truth, as Psellus said, the very sinews of the state. Rome rose—and fell—with her army.

II. *The Navy*

Republican Rome only took to the sea under compulsion; and the same is true of the Byzantine Empire. A navy had been built in the stress of the Punic Wars which was maintained to police the seas; when under the Empire the Mediterranean became a Roman lake, the navy was allowed to decay. During the third century barbarian raiders made their way down the Dardanelles, and cruised the Ægean in Rome's despite. In former days the Greek sailor had fearlessly challenged the maritime supremacy of Phœnician and Carthaginian, but when the capital was moved to the Greek East, the imperial fleet was still neglected. Constantine and Licinius might fight out their duel on shipboard, but there are no naval battles in the

Mediterranean in the fourth century. The growth of the Vandal Kingdom in Africa and its appearance as a sea power disclosed Rome's fatal weakness : Sardinia and Corsica were conquered, Italy ravaged, Rome sacked— the Vandals were masters of the Western waters. The Emperor Majorian was compelled to start anew and build a fleet, and the failure of the naval expedition against Africa in 468 was a severe blow to Roman prestige. When Justinian determined upon the reconquest of the West, he struck first at Africa : the Vandal fleet should not support the Ostrogoth against East Roman arms. But the Emperor's naval preparations were meagre : Narses was compelled to lead his forces through the pestilential marshes of Venetia, because he had not sufficient ships to transport his ten or twelve thousand men from Dalmatian Salona to Ravenna. It was, however, only with the creation of the Arab sea power and the aggressive naval policy of Moawiyā that Rome was forced once more to build a fleet in deadly earnest. This was in the main the work of Constans II, and in the seventh century there was one supreme naval command, that of the admiral (*strategos*) of the *Carabisiani*. Under him were two districts, each of which now maintained its own fleet commanded by a vice-admiral (*drungarius*), just as other provinces supported a military force. These were the province of the Cibyrrhæots—the more important—and that of the Ægean Sea, the former including Pamphylia, of old a haunt of sturdy sea-rovers and corsairs, the latter consisting of the northern coast line of Asia Minor and the islands. The fame and prestige of the navy rapidly rose at this time, but, after the last great siege of Constantinople by the Arabs, Leo III based his power upon the land army of Asia Minor, and so did his successor Constantine V. The fact that the fleet had proclaimed its vice-admiral Apsimar Emperor in 697 under the name of Tiberius III and that it had overthrown Justinian II in 713, and Anastasius II in 716 may well have been the reason, as Gelzer has suggested, for the abolition of the single supreme command : the admirals of the two naval provinces now became officers of the second rank, though possessing both civil and military jurisdiction. It was an abasement of the Navy. During the eighth century the danger of this policy might not declare itself, for the Caliphate of Bagdad did not continue the naval activity of the Caliphate of Damascus. But in the ninth century piracy was once more rife in the Mediterranean; even Scandinavian freebooters penetrated through the straits of Gibraltar, and the Pope was forced to appeal to Charlemagne to protect Corsica from the Saracens. Constantinople was no longer mistress of the Western seas. Crete and Sicily were lost to the Empire, and South Italy attacked. Michael III began a reform of the fleet, and Basil I constantly pursued an aggressive naval policy. These are the great days of Roman maritime power. A new naval province (or theme) is created, that of Samos, with its capital in Smyrna, and by the side of the ships of the three themes, there is the imperial fleet stationed at Constantinople. Smaller establishments were maintained elsewhere, in Sicily, in the Peloponnese and at the mouth of the Black Sea, while the theme of Cephallenia became the basis for Byzantine operations in the West. When the fleets acted together there was once more a single admiral in command of all the naval forces. Amongst the local fleets that of the Cibyrrhæot theme still held pride of place : here was the Empire's outpost against the Saracens, and engagements with the emirs of Adana and Tarsus were constant. If one of the emirs advanced at the head of an army, the Roman fleet, ready to sail at any moment, delivered a counterattack by sea, while the Roman land forces effected a diversion if the Saracens attempted a naval expedition : the emirs had not apparently adequate forces to resist a concerted attack on their territory both by land and water. Nicephorus Phocas could offer the support of a fleet to Liutprand, the envoy of the German Emperor Otto I, and could claim that he alone possessed any strong naval power (*navigatium fortitudo mihi soli inest*), while Constantine Porphyrogenitus incidentally speaks of the Roman mastery of the Mediterranean, from Gibraltar to the Dardanelles. But though Kekaumenos, a soldier

of the eleventh century, could still call the
fleet the glory of Romania, it was in fact
falling into decay at this time. In the
seventies the Seljuks reached the West coast
of Asia Minor, and the provinces whence
the local fleets were for the most part raised
were thrown into confusion. The central
government further had good reason to fear
the independent spirit shown by the nobles
of Asia Minor: Romanus Lecapenus having
held a naval post in the Samian theme had
risen to power as Grand Admiral, and it
may well have seemed that high naval
command offered too great temptations to
a would-be usurper. Probably both these
factors contributed to the decay of naval
efficiency.

The consequences of this short-sighted
policy were soon only too obvious. Piracy
flourished unchecked : a usurper in Asia
Minor could base his power upon the possession of a navy, could, as did Tzachas at the
end of the eleventh century, destroy Adra-
myttium and agree with the Patzinaks to
take joint action against Constantinople—
the Patzinaks were to advance by land across
the Gallipoli peninsula, while Tzachas with
his fleet would co-operate in the Dardanelles.
The monasteries on the islands became
fortresses where ammunition was stored, and
when the Normans attacked the Empire,
Rome was forced to pay the penalty of her
unpreparedness and to buy the help of the
fleet of Venice. In the ninth century she

had called on the island state in right of her suzerainty to supply ships against the Saracens of Sicily; now that assistance could only be secured by the grant of trading privileges (see ch. xiii) which jeopardised her economic independence. If Rome had maintained a " fleet in being," the Fourth Crusade might have been directed against Egypt and not against Constantinople. Though the revived Empire of the Palæologi possessed, it is true, a small but effective navy, yet the great days were past, and could not be recalled.

We cannot estimate with certainty the ordinary strength of the Byzantine navy. In the one naval expedition for which we possess detailed figures 100 ships of the imperial fleet were accompanied by 77 from the provincial fleet, while the crews were in the proportion of 23–24,000 imperial to 17,500 provincial sailors; under Michael III (858–9) it would appear that the whole naval strength available for an expedition amounted to 300 sail. The ships were manned by subjects of the Empire, by barbarians settled within the Empire, e.g. the Mardaites, and by foreign mercenaries, e.g. the Russians, who were first employed in the fleet, it seems, under the Macedonian dynasty. In the Tactica of Leo VI the crews are soldiers and sailors too, but in the expedition of 902 the soldiers are distinct from the rowers. The ships (dromonds) are for the most part built with two banks of oars, in the bow are placed the engines for hurling the fearful Greek fire :

and the crew are provided with hand grenades containing the same deadly invention, which despite oft-repeated denials does seem to have possessed explosive force. The same caution which characterises Byzantine military strategy is seen in their naval policy : the East Roman admiral only fights when the odds are in his favour, or when, for instance, to protect Roman territory an engagement is unavoidable. But there appears to be hardly any doubt that the sailors in the fleet were often unreliable, and one of an admiral's chief cares was to forestall threatened desertion.

We possess but little of the technical naval literature of the East Romans, but what has come down to us shows the same careful attention to the principles of marine warfare as to the science of military operations; Byzantine admirals studied the natural features of coast line and island, and the peculiarities of wind and tide, they elaborated a system of naval tactics and strategy, and paid as much attention as their colleagues on land to the arts of scouting and signalling. Yet despite recurrent periods of great naval efficiency the fleet never ceased to be the less distinguished service : the soldier always took precedence of the sailor, and in this, as we have seen, New Rome but preserved the traditions of the older Western capital.

CHAPTER IX

EDUCATION

For the great contest of the Christian life we ought to make every preparation that is in our power. We should company with the poets, the historians, the rhetoricians and with all men from whom we can gain any help towards the cultivation of our souls.— S. Basil in his Address to Young Students.

THE fact that Christianity had become the religion of the Empire did not carry with it any far-reaching changes in the system of education. Monks and simple priests might regard the older learning as a snare of the devil, but the leaders of the Christian Church saw no reason to break with the pagan culture of their day; and while S. Basil wrote a book for the young on the value of the study of profane authors, successive emperors showed an enlightened interest in fostering and advancing universities, in increasing the number of professors, in the foundation of libraries, and the multiplication of manuscripts of the classics. Julian the Apostate struck his heaviest blow at the Christian Church by forbidding Christians to teach in the schools. S. Basil and S. Gregory of Nazianzus had both received a university education, while Basil before his conversion had been the most brilliant pupil and intended successor of the sophist Libanius.

Let us trace in outline the education of a youth of the upper classes in the fourth century of our era.

A boy began to learn to read and write when he was five or six years old, and Christian preachers ceased not to exhort parents to realise their personal responsibility towards their children : it was in fact so easy to leave everything to the pedagogue, while insufficient care was taken to choose a fit person for this important office : Chrysostom could have wished that a monk should be selected for the duty. At ten or twelve the child turned to the study of grammar; the word, however, had a wider signification than we are accustomed to give it : it included not only a study of the declensions and conjugations, and of the rules of syntax, but a knowledge of the classics. When a passage had been read, it was then parsed and analysed, rare and difficult words explained, their etymology learned, and the meaning and literary value of the author considered. For this lexicons, paraphrases and annotated editions were employed. The pupil began with Homer, before going on to the other poets. Synesius reports proudly in one of his letters that his nephew is learning fifty verses of Homer a day, and repeats them perfectly without stumbling. A papyrus in Egypt has preserved for us a

letter from an anxious mother to her son
Ptolemy : the latter was studying under the
charge of his pedagogue with a grammarian,
but his teacher had just left : she advises
him to find a new master with the help of his
pedagogue, and not to give up his study of
Homer until he has reached the sixth book.
From a Fayum papyrus we see how the teacher
explained Homer : against each word of the
text is a translation into spoken Greek, precisely like that forbidden fruit of our early
days—those coveted literal keys to the classics.
Tragedies and comedies were also read, and
Choricius, who was a Christian, tells us that
no father had raised objection to the practice
on the score of the immoralities in the plays
of the ancient comedians. We have an echo
of a short viva voce examination in Epictetus,
where question and answer are given :
" Q. Who was Hector's father ? A. Priam.
Q. What were the names of his brothers ?
A. Alexander and Deiphobus. Q. And his
Mother's name ? A. Hekabe. Q. How do
you know this ? A. From Homer ; but Hel-
lanicus and others have written on the subject." Enough ! the scene is almost painfully
realistic.

At fourteen or fifteen the boy deserts Grammar for Rhetoric. He is still accompanied to
school by the pedagogue while a slave carries
the boy's satchel and his large and weighty
books. Even in the fourth century parents
complained about the heavy cost of school
books, and Libanius had often to point out

that they were an absolute necessity. For the study of rhetoric a large range of authors was read, mostly prose writers—Demosthenes, Herodotus, Thucydides, Isocrates and Lysias. The works of Isocrates were very popular, while much of Demosthenes and Thucydides was learned by heart. Reading aloud not only served to show whether the author was properly understood, but it also helped in the development of the voice, for in the flowing rhetoric of the day the speaker intoned rather than spoke his periods. In home work, where a boy was under the supervision of his pedagogue, much was said aloud, so that, as Libanius writes in jest, the neighbours were unable to sleep, while some had fallen ill in consequence of the noise. After the pupil had in this way become acquainted with the masters of Attic literature, written exercises were begun. The teacher read aloud a chosen example of any particular style of composition, and the scholars moulded their work on this. From the simple fable of Æsop he advanced through anecdotes to a short treatment of some famous remark or piece of proverbial wisdom; outstanding figures in history were praised, or blamed, or compared with each other, while character studies of well-known types were composed. The students might be bidden to describe the pictures in their City Council Chamber, or to discuss some general question, as Should a man marry, or not? Thus an advance was made to longer and more difficult exercises:

a speech of one of the Homeric heroes would be paraphrased in prose, and in an age when the world of culture was engrossed in its correspondence, elaborate study was needed of the art of letter-writing, and model letters were read aloud in the school; for the letter ought to represent the character of the writer, it must be short and written in pure Attic, the language should be simple, and proverbs should be frequently inserted. A recent work on the proverbs contained in the writings of Synesius shows how faithfully the prescriptions of Demetrius were followed in this respect. It is largely due to the fact that form was everything, and the content more or less immaterial that the correspondence of the period appears to us so artificial and devoid of human interest, frequently degenerating into a mere display of frigid erudition.

The human boy then as now cannot have been altogether tractable material. We see him studying under Libanius at Antioch, his pedagogue beside him with a stick ready to his hand. The sophist sits on a high chair, the scholars on low benches. Most of them came from Asia Minor, Syria and Phœnicia, and non-Attic words *would* find their way into the exercises, and the teacher's ferule and thong hardly availed to keep them out. The school year began in autumn, and lasted without any considerable break until the beginning of summer : then followed holidays for four months during the hot weather.

Lessons were given during the morning, and the elder students attended lectures in the afternoon as well. On festivals, royal birthdays, etc., the school was shut; then there were beast fights, sports and plays in the theatre. Even Christian teachers as a rule saw no harm in their pupils visiting the theatre, though Isidore of Pelusium condemned the practice. In Gaza, though the scholars were free to attend, it was the custom for the sophists to stay away. On lesser festivals, *e.g.* that in honour of Artemis, there was only one day's holiday : the boys clamoured for two days' holiday, while the parents complained that already too much time was lost from study. Every now and again there were "speech days," when the more proficient scholars or the teachers gave rhetorical displays, and friends and parents were invited. It was very difficult to maintain order on these occasions, and when the boys were called in by the slave porter they would continue singing outside, and even during the speeches would chatter between themselves about charioteers, horses and dancers, or would applaud in the wrong places. Then, as in more recent times, boys would play truant, and fights were common : provided only books and not stones were used as missiles, Libanius was prepared to wink at such encounters, but they overstepped the limits when they tossed a pedagogue in a carpet. The sophist was indeed afraid to be over-strict for fear that his pupils might desert to his rival. Even in the fourth century parents would send boys supperless to bed as a punishment, while one of the most effective disciplinary measures was to forbid the culprit to go to the public baths.

The University of Athens was still in the fourth century the most famous seat of rhetorical scholarship. To the University Athens owed whatever importance it still possessed, for otherwise it was now only a provincial town : the city fathers realised that upon the presence of the students depended the prosperity of the inhabitants, and while the state supported one sophist, the municipality paid the salary of two sophists and of at least one grammarian. The sophists were in the main foreigners, and students coming from various parts of the Empire were naturally anxious to work under their fellow-countrymen. But everywhere each teacher was in bitter hostility to his rivals, and Libanius regarded it as the duty of his scholars to make life as unpleasant as possible for his colleagues. At Athens the pupils of each sophist formed a close society; and it would have been gross treachery to their master to attend another sophist's classes. Their object was to swell the numbers of their own society, and thus increase their teacher's income and prestige. At the beginning of winter when the freshmen arrived, all the harbours of Attica were watched : the society posted its men at the Peiræus, at Sunium, and even sent them as far as Corinth to intercept the new comers. Willy nilly they were seized, and, whatever their own wishes might have been, were kept close prisoners until they had sworn to enrol themselves as pupils of the particular sophist whose cause their captors had espoused. Libanius wanted to study under his fellow-countryman Epiphanius, but he was made prisoner and forced to yield by the scholars of Diophantus who violently carried him off from another band who had first laid hands on him. On the following morning the freshman was taken to the baths, where he was ducked and formally enrolled, and then had to give a banquet to his fellow-scholars. Rivalry between societies was such that regular battles with clubs and stones and swords were fought in the streets of Athens. An unpopular sophist had mud thrown in his face in the street, while another, an Egyptian, was dragged out of bed at night, and was hurried off to a fountain into which the students threatened to throw him if he would not swear to leave Athens forthwith. Then, as now, ball games were played with enthusiasm and work often suffered : while many a student ran into debt through squandering money on fair prostitutes. But friendships were formed which were life-long, and old men loved to recall the days which they had spent in youth in the violet-crowned city.

The study of philosophy, which would begin with the eighteenth or twentieth year, was the crown of fourth-century education, and though elsewhere, as at Alexandria and Constantinople, the state supported the teachers, at Athens the funds of the Academy, increased by the gifts of former scholars, were sufficient for the needs of the professors who were thus rendered independent. Aristotle was studied as an introduction to Plato, and the understanding of Plato's works necessitated a general acquaintance with the principles of mathematics, geometry, music and astronomy; well-tried text-books, some of them dating from the second century, still held their place. Thus Proclus in the fifth century lectured on Euclid, though many thought that the work of Ptolemæus was more satisfactory. The writings of Aristotle and Plato were read through in a fixed order; it seems that Proclus would deliver as many as five lectures daily, and in each lecture would cover about one and a half pages of the Teubner text. But it was not only Aristotle and Plato who were studied. The father of Themistius lectured on Pythagoras, Zeno, and Epicurus, though Epicurus would seem only to have served as a butt for ridicule; Themistius himself at Constantinople did not exclude the study of the Stoics from his courses. The teacher had to his hand a number of serviceable explanations of Aristotle (ἐξηγήσεις); but Themistius seems to have been an innovator in writing for his classes paraphrases of the works of Plato and Aristotle : these became known through the notes of students, so that the philosopher, like Blackstone at a later day, found himself compelled to publish them in self defence. Part of his paraphrase of Aristotle we still possess.

But the outstanding feature of the teaching of Themistius is its insistence on the ethical and practical value of philosophy, and in this he was supported by the Emperor. He was himself a statesman as well as a professor, and he sought to bring philosophy from her cloistered retreat and make her a power in the moral education of good citizens. Indeed the age regarded physical science with suspicion; the cosmogony of the Christian was once for all revealed in the Bible, and it was easy to slip into heretical views. Even Greek metaphysics were suspect. Themistius in Constantinople in one of his speeches complains that if anyone gives himself to the study of Aristotle there are always folk to call the attention of the authorities to the criminal, and if he writes on Syllogisms or Physics he deserves death without a doubt. The spirit which at Alexandria hounded Hypatia to her death was widespread. Thus it was on the neutral ground of logic that Christian and pagan tended to concentrate their study, and Alexandria, where the Christian philosopher Origen had founded his great catechetical school, bore the palm from the City of Athene. The philosophical school of Alexandria indeed lasted on until the eve of the Arab invasion.

Such in outline was the course of Roman education in the fourth and fifth centuries. Schools were spread throughout the Roman

East; at Nicomedia and Ancyra in Asia Minor, at Cæsarea in Cappadocia, and at New Cæsarea in Pontus; in Cilicia and Pamphylia schools are mentioned, and at Sardes and Pergamon in Ionia. For the south Alexandria was the centre, whence teachers were drawn for the schools at Pelusium, Hermupolis and Oxyrynchos and for those of Cæsarea in Palestine and of Emesa on the Arabian border. The Christian school of rhetoric at Gaza established in the fifth century a reputation throughout the East, while in Syria Antioch, Apamea, Chalkis and Emesa boasted famous teachers.

In all these towns the Greek language held its own; the greatest teachers, such as Themistius and Libanius, looked down with scorn upon the western tongue. Libanius refused of set purpose to learn a word of Latin, and regarded the inception of a school of Latin in Antioch as a personal affront. Only where Roman law was taught was the study of Latin vigorously pursued; elsewhere the efforts of the Emperors to extend its use were in the main unsuccessful. But at the law schools of Alexandria and Berytus sophistic lost ground, and only so much rhetoric was learned as was practically useful for the pleader or administrator. Justinian sought to revive the study of law, which was henceforth restricted to the Universities of Constantinople, Rome and Berytus. The course was in future to cover five years. Undergraduates in their first year read the

Institutes and books 1 to 4 of the Digest; the three following years were spent on the Digest, though the students were not examined on books 37 to 50; the fifth year was devoted to the Code. The Emperor at the same time severely forbade the " ragging " of freshers, which he considered an unworthy and detestable practice, fit only for slaves, and not for serious students.

Even in the fourth century, as we have seen, the old culture was already on the defensive; orthodox Emperors became less and less tolerant of Greek philosophy. In 529 Justinian confiscated the funds from which the teaching of philosophy was supported at Athens, while the professors themselves went into banishment in Persia. The culture of the East Roman world must be drawn from Christian sources. Procopius levels at Justinian a general charge of diverting to other ends the money which his predecessors had expended on the salaries of doctors and teachers. The barbarian Phocas (602–610) closed the University in Constantinople, and under his successor Heraclius an ecclesiastical school took its place; to this new academy, housed in a palace near the Chalkoprateia, the Emperor summoned Stephanus, the last representative of the philosophical school of Alexandria. Henceforth, it would seem, education in the capital always remained under the control of the Patriarch.

The ninth century saw a revival of learning in philosophy and science which was warmly

F

supported by the Emperors. The Cæsar Bardas refounded the old university of Constantinople, and professors of geometry, astronomy and philology were appointed, while from the Bibliotheca of Photius we can gauge the wide range of prose authors studied and analysed by the indefatigable reading circle of these Byzantine encyclopædists. Classical learning indeed never ceased to be cultivated in Constantinople from the time of Photius to the fall of the city in 1204, but it was regarded with suspicion by the Church, and Alexius I Comnenus in his reform of education, although encouraging those who had obtained some rudimentary knowledge of the philosophy of Aristotle, yet found it necessary to urge that the first place should be given to the study of the Bible.

Of instruction in law we hear but little, but we know that in the eleventh century there was no provision made in Constantinople for legal education : when in 1045 under Constantine Monomachus a new school was founded in the capital, the Emperor was forced to confess that his predecessors had left " the sacred study of the law to drift as chance might carry it, like a rudderless boat in the midst of the sea of life." Barristers had begun to practice without any course of study, and even for those who were willing to work there were only text-books and no teachers. It is clear, however, from the wording of the Emperor's extremely interesting instrument of foundation that there were still public

" grammarians " teaching in Constantinople, and it is instructive to note that it was necessary for the president of the new law school (νομοφύλαξ) to be versed alike in Greek and Latin.

Unfortunately it would seem that the school which had begun with such promise enjoyed but a short life, and in the troublous days of the later eleventh century the Treasury can have had little money to spare for education. The Empire, which could not support its own navy, doubtless regarded a university as a luxury which must be forgone under the stern constraint of war.

CHAPTER X

LITERATURE

We need a Christian and a pagan schooling : from the one we gain profit for the soul, from the other we learn the witchery of words.—Choricius, Second Speech on Bishop Marcian of Gaza. (Ed. Boissonade, p. 109.)

ROME had conquered the states which had arisen out of the Asiatic Empire of Alexander the Great, but she had never succeeded in imposing Latin civilisation upon the lands which bordered the Eastern Mediterranean : the Hellenistic culture was too widespread and too firmly rooted. Despite the efforts of Diocletian and his successors to foster the language of the West, the Greek speech held its own, and though it adopted many Latin words from the vocabulary of law and administration, together with a large number of military terms, it was only the official formulæ of the imperial chancery which in rescript and edict exercised a lasting influence on Greek style. Thus, the literature of East Rome is a Greek literature, even the Latin epics of the African Corippus (sixth century) follow Greek models. It is also a learned literature. The Byzantines inherited the traditions of Hel-

lenistic scholars—men who had sought not so
much to interpret the life of their own day
as to recover the thought and achievement of
the glorious past—who moulded their style
on an Attic idiom which had to be acquired
with the aid of lexicon and grammar. Thus
arose the cleavage which still exists in Greece
between the spoken and the written language.
What is true of the students of the time of
the Ptolemies holds good for the " Christian Alexandrines " of Constantinople. Their
works lack spontaneity; each literary revival
looks backward, and serves only to draw
more tightly the threads which linked the
present with the past : it is but marked by a
closer imitation of that Attic style which
had become archaic and artificial. Christian
authors thus stand aloof from their own age;
composing their works in and for a Christian
society, they yet speak of Christian practices
and festivals as of things unknown and
strange : we seem to hear once more Herodotus explaining for his Greek readers the
amazing cults of Egyptian worship. Pagan
conceptions of chance and fate recur in their
pages as motive powers in a world which prided
itself upon its Chalcedonian orthodoxy; to
the despair of the modern ethnologist peoples
which an earlier Greece never knew are
christened with names which had been canon-
ised by the great historians of classical times.
We to-day are ready enough to sacrifice formal
perfection, if only we can catch the expression of authentic personality. To the typical

Byzantine form was all important : only by
loyal adherence to a secular tradition could
he read his title clear to a place in the temple
of Literature. Thus East Rome guarded
scrupulously its priceless heritage : it studied
it in commentaries and paraphrases, but it no
longer possessed the divine curiosity of youth,
the passion to fathom the secret of Nature
and of the Universe, that free spirit of inquiry
which blows like a morning breeze through
the works of the early Greek thinkers. Byzantine literature showed its greatest originality
in theology, sacred poetry and history, though
the epigram still lived, and it is to the interest
of the Byzantines in this form of literary art
that we owe the preservation of the Greek
Anthology.[1]

We saw that in the social and religious life
of the Empire the age of Constantine marks
an epoch; and this is no less true of literary
form. A new principle makes its appearance :
classical poetry had been governed by laws of
quantity, its structure was determined by the
length of its syllables; but the spoken language was now governed by accent; the stress
fell upon the accented syllable, and thus
unaccented syllables, whatever their natural
length might be, were shortened. This new
principle was adopted by Gregory of Nazianzus,
who wrote poetry of which the structure is
determined by accent alone, while Christian

[1] The whole of the Greek Anthology can now be
read in Mr. Paton's English translation. (Loeb
Library. Heinemann, 1916 to 1918.)

hymns were composed in accentuated verse, the lines being linked together by the introduction of rhyme; further, inasmuch as rhetoric with its rythmic cadences tended to break down the distinction between prose and verse, prose writing was also affected by the new development. But since the literature of New Rome was essentially conservative, the supremacy of quantitative poetry was never seriously threatened, though accent continually influenced its structure, and gave a new effect to the old metres. It is a striking example of the force of a literary tradition.

In the fourth century were produced the works of Athanasius, the champion of orthodoxy, of Basil, the founder of Greek Monasticism, of the theologians Gregory of Nazianzus and Gregory of Nyssa, and of John Chrysostom the exegete, while, shortly after, Cyril of Alexandria published his dogmatic and polemical treatises. For all later Byzantine theology these were the great decisive authorities; it was not sought to go behind them to the earlier Greek literature of the sub-apostolic age. Arethas of Cæsarea (tenth century), who studied the Christian apologists of the second and third centuries, remained an exception, and his innovation had no permanent influence on subsequent thought. Here too the fourth century marks the parting of the ways.

But the great writers of the Age of the Fathers had no intention of breaking entirely with that classical tradition in which they had been educated. They devoted to the service of Christianity the rhetoric which they had learned from the pagan sophists. Their highly coloured style is the product of the schools, and just as the brilliant periods of a Libanius were interrupted by the applause of his hearers, so were the sermons of the orators of the church. One point of difference, however, must not be overlooked : while the sophist declaimed on academic themes to the cultured few, the Christian preacher appealed with his living message to the poor and illiterate, the populace of the great cities. For modern readers it is precisely this florid splendour of diction which tends to produce a sense of monotony : a purple patch in a sermon, though inartistic, may be forgiven, but when the whole texture of the address is a radiant mosaic of purple patches, the mind wearies and no true climax can be attained. Further, to us of the West the Greek fathers appear to forget that the half is often greater than the whole; the East is tolerant of many words, and Asian influences are clearly discernible in the wealth of imagery and elaboration which at times rather obscures than illuminates. But this is not to say, as would some modern scholars, that Byzantine literature is everywhere dominated by Oriental characteristics : to the present writer this view is an exaggeration : to him it would appear more important to accentuate New Rome's literary relations with that cosmopolitan civilisation which developed after

Alexander's death on the shores of the Levant, and particularly in the great Egyptian city which the Conqueror founded. This civilisation incontestably absorbed much from the Orient, but it remained essentially Greek, and it is this Hellenistic legacy which, so far as the author can see, remained the principal source of inspiration for Byzantine literature.

But granted that the work of the fourth century fathers is too decorative and too little disciplined, granted that it may be difficult for the modern student to view with other than a smile of pity the sight of Europe distracted over a diphthong, yet if we can rid ourselves of our prepossession, this literature remains intensely human; as we read it, we shall feel again the burning zeal for righteousness which consumed Chrysostom, and the courage which would bring hope to despairing Antioch when after an hour of inconsiderate tumult the whole city awaited the royal vengeance; through the letters of Basil we shall renew acquaintance with the manly valour of an ecclesiastical statesman upon whom rested the heavy burden of the care of the churches; and forgetting that shameless howl of triumph with which Gregory of Nazianzus greeted the death of Julian, we shall turn to the verses in which he painted the intimate joys and sorrows of his own chequered life.

But this humanity is sadly to seek in the polemical writings to which the Monophysite controversy gave birth; they will continue to

F 2

be studied by the historian and theologian, but the general reader will seek elsewhere his pleasure. Yet it was about the year 500 that there lived the unknown author who sought to persuade men that his works came from the pen of Dionysius the Areopagite, Paul's disciple. He had his desire : only of recent years has the date of their composition been placed beyond controversy.

Previously the two worlds of Greek and Christian thought had lived on side by side, now the ancient culture is fused with the new faith. The mystical treatises of the Areopagite, drawn in large measure from the writings of Proclus the Neo-Platonist, enlisted Greek philosophy in the defence of Christianity. The old feud was buried, while in the seventh century Maximus, the champion of orthodoxy in the Monothelitic controversy, only assured the position of the Dionysiac teaching in the Eastern Church. Leontius of Byzantium had already (sixth century) introduced into Christian speculation the definitions of Aristotle.

The Iconoclastic controversy caused John of Damascus to write his renowned defence of the sacred images, and in " The Fountain of Knowledge ". he sought to co-ordinate and systematise the legacy of the Fathers of the Church. " I will say nothing of my own," he avows : originality is already suspect. The Festival of Orthodoxy (843) may be said to mark the close of the creative period of Byzantine theology : it heralds the era of traditionalism. The thought of the Church ceases to possess its old receptivity; it will admit no further infiltration of the ideas of Greek philosophy; thus the humanists of East Rome fall, like the heretics, under ecclesiastical condemnation. But none the less Aristotle, Plato, Proclus and Iamblichus were still studied. John Byzantios, who could compare Plato to Christ, was the master of Psellos, who saw in Plato a precursor of Christianity : John Italos under Alexius I was the pupil of Psellos, and admitting metempsychosis and the Platonic doctrine of ideas, was condemned for preferring Platonism to orthodoxy. It was another pupil of Psellos who in his enthusiasm for the older world threw himself off a rock into the sea with the cry "Take me, Poseidon." Thus we can hardly wonder that Alexius I in undertaking a reform of education in the capital felt it necessary to insist that more attention should be paid to the Bible than to pagan literature, and we begin to understand why the unknown author of the tenth-century satire, "The True Patriot" (the "Philopatris"), finds his traitors in those who wished for the defeat of the Roman forces in Asia and in the *humanists of Byzantium :* it is the same alliance of orthodoxy and the imperial power, of church and army, which we have constantly had occasion to notice.

It was only when East Roman theology, absorbed in the barren controversy with Rome, had ceased to be productive that it won fresh victories in the West. Scotus

Erigena in the ninth century translated into Latin the works of Pseudo-Dionysius and of Maximus; Peter Lombard, the first systematic theologian of the Middle Ages in Western Europe, took for his model " The Fountain of Knowledge " of John of Damascus, and the champion of Image-worship also exercised considerable influence upon Thomas Aquinas. In the East the Syriac and Armenian literatures are for the most part fed by translations from the Greek, while Bulgaria by her early versions of Byzantine works created a library which Serbia and Russia alike adapted to their own uses.

In secular poetry Byzantium never attained to any first class achievement; the hexameter died with the Egyptian Nonnus (fourth-fifth century), and thereafter it is the twelve-syllabled verse which is regularly employed. Of this George of Pisidia (seventh century) was the master who served as model for later writers. From his poems rather than from any other source can the student learn what East Roman sovereignty meant for the citizen of Constantinople. But Byzantine secular poetry can show no works planned on a large scale : just as art won some of its greatest triumphs in " Kleinkunst "—reliefs in ivory, mosaic, goldsmith's work—so it was in verse : the epigram alone is cultivated with outstanding success. Lyric poetry dies : the mutual love of man and woman is banished to the popular epic. Byzantine literature as we possess it to-day sprang from two sources :

from the idealists of the monastery and the
nunnery with their thoughts on another world,
seeking in this present life but an opportunity
for its renunciation, and from the realists of
the court—statesmen, emperors, bureaucrats.
Romance thus became either sinful or incon-
venient, because incalculable, and literary
conservatism was loath to acknowledge the
charm of the peasant's song.

But in religious poetry Byzantium produced
at least one writer of real originality. Romanus (early sixth century), converted from
Judaism, was ordained deacon in Beirut, and
from Syria came to Constantinople, where
during a nocturnal festival in the church at
Blachernæ he was given by a miracle (so ran
the legend) the gift of hymn-writing. In form
Romanus may have found his models in
the Syriac hymns of his fellow-countryman
Ephraem; just as dialogue is frequent in the
works of Ephraem, so Romanus introduced it
into his hymns, which would then perhaps be
sung antiphonally by two distinct choirs.
He celebrated the glories of the saints and
martyrs, and the praises of the Christian
mysteries. Unfortunately we can only obtain
an inadequate idea of his work, for many of the
hymns are still unpublished. The very clarity
and simplicity of style of his best compositions
caused them to be neglected or banished from
the service books. After the ninth century
they were superseded by more learned and
elaborate " Canons," and the life and vigour
of the early promise were extinguished.

It is, however, in the sphere of history that later Roman literature most clearly shows its superiority over that of the West. Despite periods when, as in the seventh century, the sword had perforce to take the place of the pen, the classical tradition never died, and to the last the Eastern Empire studied and recorded its own history and that of its friends and foes. We are only slowly beginning to realise how great is our debt to Clio of the Byzantines.

And by the side of the literary narrative of the historian there runs also the unending series of more or less popular universal chronicles which take into their view, not merely the story of Greece and Rome, but that of the whole world, so far as it was known, from the creation of man down to the days of the " very sinful " monk who compiled the record. The interest of these chronicles lies in the width of their scope; a world-salvation has given rise to a world-history : it is only modern archæological discovery that has found their scheme too narrow, and a Maspero and an Eduard Meyer have but adapted to the new knowledge which the spade of the excavator has recovered that idea of a continuous development in the story of mankind which formed the foundation of the Christian chronography of the Eastern Empire.

And the chronicle, the people's history-book, leads finally to a mention of the popular literature of the Byzantine world. This consists mainly of old Greek legends which have undergone enlargement and adaptation: the story of the Siege of Troy, the chronicle of the achievements of Alexander the Great now become the type of a Christian hero; of far-travelled Eastern tales hardly recognizable in their Christian dress: the history of Barlaam and Josaphat, the most famous of all, may now be read in an English translation; of epics sung by the camp fire on frontier forays against the paynim Saracen: as the epic of Digenis Akritas, only recovered in the last century; and perhaps most interesting of all, of saints' lives written by humble monks for simple folk, and serving to recall to us the joys, the griefs and heroisms of the common men and women whose doings were too unimportant to figure in the histories of the Empire. From this popular literature of Byzantium much could be gained: the fields are white already to harvest.

CHAPTER XI

BYZANTINE ART

" The pictured image leads the mind to memory of celestial things."—NILUS, *Greek Anthology*, Book I, no. 33.

THERE are many excellent reasons why this chapter should be brief, but one alone would suffice. For the present writer to adventure any independent judgment on the thorny problems raised by the study of Byzantine Art would be an impertinence: nothing less. This chapter, let it be avowed forthwith, is quarried from the works of the acknowledged masters; to these it may perhaps serve as a humble signpost; it is, in fact, a preface to the bibliography (see p. 251).[1]

Christian art was born in the catacombs; driven underground by the pagan state, it was a symbolic art: its frescoes never sought to depict historical events, but through the mystic signs which the Greek cities of the Near East had created—the East whence Christianity had sprung—it interpreted to itself its message of cheer, its " good spell " of

[1] I gratefully acknowledge the criticism and help of my friend Mr. Stroud Read.

salvation. Thus from this present evil world
the despised sect turned for confidence and
encouragement to the world of the spirit.
The Alexandrian motives of the anchor and
the dove received a new meaning. Hermes
with the ram on his shoulder became the
Good Shepherd bearing the lost sheep, while
Psyche and Orantes praying amidst the flowers
of Paradise were figures of the sure and certain
hope of the soul's immortality. With the
victory of the persecuted Galilæans in the
fourth century art rose, like Demeter, from
the underworld to deck the triumph of Christianity. Everywhere under royal favour
churches came into being, as though by magic,
and for their embellishment the old symbolism
seemed too slight, too wistful. The winter
was past, and spring called for pageantry.

In the first centuries of our era pagan
Rome had created out of Hellenistic art an
imperial art, realistic and monumental,
stamped with the Roman mark, spreading
through the provinces with the universalism
of her Empire : and as the City of Rome
decayed in the third century, and the East,
as we have seen, reasserted its supremacy, this
imperial tradition found in the East the colour
and the decorative skill in which to clothe
imperial pomp. To the fresco was added an
extended use of the wall-mosaic, an art working for broader and larger effects, with sharper
outlines, an art to be viewed at a distance, a
spacious art, needing for its development the
co-operation of the architect. But the new

capital was set in Greek-speaking lands, and
alongside of this Oriental art of decoration and
of colour, Greek humanism and the great
types of human beauty which Hellenism had
created still exercised a mighty influence.
Constantinople might be an upstart city
without traditions, but it claimed for itself
the splendour of the classical past : into it
were collected not only the sacred relics of the
Christian faith, but also the masterpieces of
the pagan world. New Rome became a
museum, an unmatched school of art. At the
same time the Church had a great story to
tell : she wished to record with pride the
heroism of the faithful departed and the
loyalty of the martyrs in face of torture and
death. Not only so : the walls of her sanctuaries should become for the illiterate con-
verts an illustrated Bible, a pictured history
of redemption. Just when in East and West
alike a purely ornamental and decorative art
seemed about to triumph, the Christian
Church, dropping her early prejudices, joined
with the state in accepting the legacy of
Hellas, and by her influence preserved for the
world an art which could still express human
personality with its depth of religious and
emotional sentiment. The Saviour had
assumed the form and nature of man, and by
so doing had given an untold value to human
individuality. The Church refused to rest
content with ornament alone. In that complex art of New Rome there was indeed room
for all : for the picturesque motives of the

school of Alexandria—for nature with her vine tendrils and her acanthus leaves, for pagan scenes of sport and country-side, for animals and the games of naked children by the river, for all the play of Hellenistic fancy : there was room for the Roman tradition of processional pageantry, of pomp and power : room for the lavish colour and magnificence of Persian decoration and arabesque, and room too for those types of human nobility that Greece had created, while in architecture the Empire took what the East could give and raised it to a new potency, until it flowered in the world wonder of Justinian's church of the Holy Wisdom.

It is indeed the complexity of this art which creates the difficulty of the so-called " Byzantine question " : for in the search for origins students are easily led to claim exclusive importance for one particular locality : Orient *or* Rome, Hellas *or* the East. The Byzantine world drew from many wells, and at times it seems to the historical student that art critics have hardly realised how many-sided was the receptivity of the Eastern Empire; New Rome borrowed freely from other peoples, but yet, nowhere truer to the traditions of old Rome than in this, set her own impress on that which she had borrowed, until it took new form and shape under her hand. All, however, that can here be attempted is to mark the successive stages in Byzantine artistic development.

In the fourth and fifth centuries Con-

stantinople was but one among many centres
from which influences radiated. Egypt,
Palestine, Syria, Asia Minor were rivals to
the capital. The buildings of Constantine at
Jerusalem became known far and wide through
pilgrims streaming to the Holy Land and
bearing back with them mementoes of the
sacred places which they had visited. Antioch through its traders carried Syrian
decorative art to the furthest coasts of the
Mediterranean, while the architects of Asia
Minor, adopting the dome—possibly from
Persia—sought to develop in brick the possibilities of this Eastern form. But just as the
fifth century saw the triumph of centralisation
in matters ecclesiastical, so gradually the
influence of Constantinople grew in the sphere
of art; and this was due not so much to the
export of wrought capitals of Proconnesian
marble as to two facts: that many centres
sought for their churches and for their civil
buildings imperial grants, and he who pays
the piper calls the tune, and that the Emperors consciously desired this extension of
the influence of the capital, so that the imperial will supplies an impulse which carried
Asiatic methods throughout the Empire.
The Emperor's architects, drawn from many
centres, yet tended as servants of a common
master to pursue common ends, and by the
time of Justinian Constantinople need fear
no rival : the West copied the Churches of
New Rome as it had formerly followed the
fashion set by Jerusalem.

Sancta Sophia, consecrated in 537, was five years in building, and the whole Empire was put under contribution for Justinian's masterpiece. Its architects Anthemius of Tralles and Isidore of Miletus both came from Asia Minor, and while from the East Constantinople might derive the cupola and the decorative scheme of multi-coloured marble, yet we may surely trace Greek subtlety in the masterly use of the pendentive, whereby on a rectangular basis the circular cupola might rise with such grace that it appeared rather to be suspended from Heaven. God and man, contemporaries felt, had co-operated in this marvellous building, for if from God came the skill of the architects, it was the Emperor who had chosen them for the creation of this building, alive in all its parts : for here Byzantine art, scorning the dead weight of sheer mass, " sought in the play of thrusts a new equilibrium."

In this First Golden Age of East Roman artistic achievement by the side of a majestic symbolism which had replaced the simple imagery of the catacombs (cf. S. Apollinare in Classe at Ravenna) mosaic elaborated the splendour of a new historical realism, as in S. Vitale at Ravenna, and, greatly daring, introduced new themes, such as the passion of Christ, which an earlier age had hesitated to portray. At this period are formed the types of sacred iconography, of Christ and the Virgin, of prophets and apostles, while a profane art, which unfortunately has perished, celebrated the imperial triumphs of Justinian and his generals.

With the seventh century East Rome had neither time nor money to spend on art : all her energies were absorbed in the task of self-preservation, but with the Iconoclast Emperors art gains new life. For the Iconoclasts, it must be repeated, were not opponents of art as such, but only of a particular form of art. While the historical style of the age of Justinian tends to decay, the Emperors encouraged a profane and naturalistic art—an art which to a large extent sought its inspiration in the past. The artists turned to the countryside and to animal life, to the city and the hippodrome, and to the realism of portraiture. At the same time in their additions to the imperial palace we can trace the Oriental magnificence of the Moslem court of Bagdad, while to the East also is due the introduction of work in cloisonnée enamel.

The fire of persecution awoke the monks to fresh vigour in religious painting. The miniature artists gained a new freedom : they too became realists, and, interpreting biblical metaphors with a literalism which is at times humorous, they appealed to the people with a vigorous pictured polemic against the Iconoclasts. But the triumph of the monk and of the sacred image had a double effect on Byzantine sacred art : it tended to hallow those traditional forms which had been attacked, and thus to perpetuate a fixed iconography, and it also strengthened monastic influences: the monastery of Studius became the vigorous centre of a cloistral art.

With the dynasties of the Macedonian and Comnenian sovereigns East Rome entered on a Second Age of Gold. External expansion, internal prosperity and intellectual vigour are accompanied by a splendid artistic revival. Basil I inaugurates this renaissance by the creation of his New Church, and the dominant type in religious architecture takes the form of a Greek cross enclosed in a square building, so that the arms of the cross do not appear in the external structure as they had done in the cruciform churches of the fifth and sixth centuries. Formerly the scheme of marble decoration had been in the main confined to the interior of the Church : now a wealth of rich polychrome ornament in brick or marble covers the outside walls—a change doubtless suggested by the fact that the immense flat surfaces of the great Byzantine buildings were generally devoid of structural ornament or plastic decoration, and thus there was needed some striking compensation for this absence of relief. These new methods were a further victory of Oriental colouristic art. Even in domestic architecture houses of Roman type have given place to those built on Eastern models, faced with colonnaded porticoes. It is still a disputed question how far the development of Armenian architecture at this time determines, or is determined by the new Byzantine style. Once more in the revival of profane art the influence of antiquity asserts itself, and the cycles of legend which clustered round Achilles and Alexander provided themes for East Roman craftsmen. The triumphs of the imperial armies fostered a historical art which is keenly interested in portraiture; both tendencies, the classical and the realistic, are reflected in the works of ecclesiastical artists; portraying Eastern scenes they had ample material from which to choose their models, for tenth-century Constantinople was a great ethnological museum, where all races met.

But the outstanding feature of the period is the elaboration of that iconography which from henceforth was to dominate Byzantine sacred art. The issue of the Iconoclast controversy had been the triumph of dogma, and the decoration of the Churches now became a systematic exposition of the orthodox creed. In the narthex and the nave is pictured the cycle of the great Christian festivals, and here are ranged the armies of the faithful, victory-crowned—saints, monks, martyrs and bishops. From the world of sense one passes into the sanctuary, where the institution of the Eucharist typifies the greatest mystery of the Church Terrestrial : thence the artist ascends to the apse figuring the celestial church, where is enthroned the Mother of God " higher than the Heavens " : finally, far above in the main cupola of the church, the whole is dominated by the Incarnate image of God, Christ the Lord of all, combining in his Consubstantial Person the Divine Son and the Ancient of Days Who, as even iconodules were prepared to allow, could not be represented by the hands of mortals. Such is the supreme expression of the heart of the Church of the Seven Councils.

After the recapture of Constantinople in 1261 there was yet another renaissance in Byzantine art, though here in the impoverished world of the Palæologi the work was less sumptuous. But this revival, save for the church of the Virgin of the Chora, bore its finest fruit outside the capital, in Serbia (see ch. xiv), in Greece at Mistra, and in the Athos Monasteries. The Church had thrown in its lot with the state, and when the state was reborn, then the Church took fresh life, and art with the Church was inspired anew.

The question of the influence of Byzantine art upon the west of Europe has as yet received no complete answer, but scholars are now in agreement that the method of attack must be found in a detailed study for which each region and each period will present a separate problem : only thus will it be safe to form general statements. It is, however, clear that there were many channels through which the West maintained communication with the East Roman Empire and the further Orient. The pilgrim and the trader were links of connection between the two worlds, as were the Greek artist and the Greek craftsman executing commissions in barbarian lands; the Basilian monk and the Oriental bishop invaded the West : it was from Tarsus in Cilicia that S. Theodore came to Canterbury. Thus in the fifth and sixth centuries Italian and Gallic monasticism was an Egyptian institution, following Eastern rules and owing its inspiration to immigrants from the shores of the Levant. Eastern saints were venerated in the West : over the porches of Roman shops could be seen statuettes of S. Simeon Stylites, serving as talismans to guard the inmates; from the East came precious relics, such as the cross sent by Justin II to Rome and still preserved in the Vatican which contained a fragment of the Sacred Wood; the West adopted festivals from the Eastern liturgy—the Dormition of the Virgin, the Exaltation of the Cross—while Gregory of Tours derived from Syrian merchants such legends as those of the Seven Sleepers of Ephesus, or of S. Thomas and his mission to India. The cosmopolitan church needed ornaments and sacred utensils for her ceremonies and ritual; she required a figure-art for the representation of biblical scenes; thus she drew textiles from Tyre and Berytus, carved capitals from Proconnesus, manuscripts and ivories from Alexandria and Antioch, while Syria furnished her with new themes for sacred paintings, for example, the Crucifixion, at times to the scandal of Western worshippers.

In Italy after Justinian's reconquest Ravenna became a Byzantine city, while in Rome there grew up a powerful oriental colony which was reinforced by exiled monks fleeing from the Iconoclast persecution. Thus both Rome and Ravenna drew their artistic inspiration from the East. Only when the Papacy turned for support to the Franks was this influence weakened. Southern Italy— the Magna Graecia of earlier times—largely retained its Greek character, and this became only more marked when Constantine V added Calabria to the theme of Sicily, and when the victories of the Macedonian sovereigns re-established Byzantine supremacy in these lands. In the latter part of the eleventh century Desiderius, abbot of Monte Cassino, called in Greek artists to decorate his church with mosaic and marble work, and imported from the East bronze, gold, silver and enamelled ornaments. These Greek crafts-men inspired a native Benedictine school, which soon freed itself from foreign control. In the early twelfth century under the Norman rulers Byzantine and Saracenic art flourished side by side, while through Venice in the north, which had taken the place of Ravenna, Rome in the thirteenth century procured Greek craftsmen, and here Byzantine influence continued as late as the fourteenth century.

The renaissance of art under Charlemagne owed much to Eastern models—to miniatures and textile fabrics—while the cathedral at Aachen is built in the form of those churches of the Orient which commemorated the martyrs of the faith. It is still a hotly dis-puted question how much Romanesque archi-tecture owes to the art of the East, while the cupolas of the churches of Périgord would appear to be derived from Oriental sources, though here again the problem of origins is still undetermined. In Cologne from the ninth century onward the construction of the churches shows clear traces of Eastern influence, while in Languedoc and Provence Western sculptors in their statues of Christ and in decorative motives, such as the acanthus leaf, translated Greek painting into carved stone.

When the East Roman princess Theophano married the son of the Emperor Otto the Great (972) she brought with her to Germany "countless wealth of treasure": Greek monks lived in German monasteries, and at the German court there were probably Greek architects, as well as Greek counsellors. This foreign influence only grew in strength under the later Ottonian sovereigns. It centred in the school of Regensburg in the eleventh century, and can be traced in the sculpture of Bamberg. It reached its height in the thirteenth century, when the Crusaders had carried to the West the wonders of the Orient. It has been suggested that the sudden advance in the plastic art of Hildesheim in the years 1190–1210 may be ultimately derived from the study of Eastern models. Thus through the early middle ages the art of Byzantium penetrated and inspired Europe, until the West became master of its own means of self-expression.

The civil art of East Rome is almost entirely lost to us, but much of what was most characteristic of the Byzantine Empire—the art of the Church—remains. The supreme artistic achievement of Constantinople is its architecture with its glorious sense of colour in wall mosaic and marble revetment, and next to this its exquisite technical perfection in what must be called the " minor " arts : ivory-carving and miniature painting, enamel work and the production of fabric designs. Byzantine art has often been scorned as decadent and lifeless; [1] but of recent years there has been manifest a growing appreciation of its permanent value and significance.[2] Why does the beauty of this art still move us ? How came it to transcend the limitations of its ancestry—the somewhat pompous heaviness of Roman imperial art, the triviality of Hellenistic art, the monotony of the art of the East ? The secret surely lies in a religious enthusiasm which did not exhaust itself either in asceticism or dogma, but spent its reserves of energy in the expression of beauty—in the purity of line and colour. Retaining his Hellenic legacy of an art that was not confined to a decorative symbolism, inheriting those majestic types which had early become traditional in the iconography of the Eastern Church, the Byzantine was never distracted by his search for originality of theme, never tempted to think that in mere verisimilitude lay the artist's goal—he was free to create the

[1] So D. Maillart : *L'Art byzantin*. Paris (1924).
[2] In England the turn of the tide was marked by Clive Bell's *Art*. London, 1914.

imperishable forms of his ecstatic vision. And thus before the masterpieces of that creative genius we to-day are conscious not primarily of any technical achievement, but rather of a religious emotion which art has immortalised. The East Roman ascetic, driven by his enthusiasm into the wilderness, craved a calm of soul which was not of this world's giving; its fruits: joy, courage, power; that which the anchorite often failed to win from his desert solitude the artist found in beauty, for at the heart of that passion which inspired Byzantine art there is peace. The Byzantine artist was content to accept and to perpetuate the stately religious tradition once delivered to him by the Fathers, for in and through that tradition he found that which he sought—the peace that passeth understanding.

CHAPTER XII

LATER ROMAN LAW

Thine, Roman, be the task to rule the nations with thy sway : these shall be thine arts—to impose the law of peace, to spare the humbled and to crush the proud.—VIRGIL, *Aeneid*, VI, 851–3.

THE Law of Rome is at once the most original achievement of the Roman genius and its greatest gift to posterity. Through the centuries Roman discipline and Roman conservatism raised and safeguarded this imperishable monument. To many who know nothing of Byzantine history the name of Justinian the lawgiver is familiar as a household word. If we would trace the development of that law under the East Roman Emperors, we may distinguish four main periods : (i) the period of codification beginning under Diocletian and culminating in the work of Justinian, (ii) the legislation of the Iconoclast sovereigns, (iii) the return to the law as formulated by Justinian under the Macedonian monarchs, and (iv) the period of decline. We must very briefly consider the principal features of each of these stages in the later history of Roman Law, remembering that law is now the expression of the monarch's will : the autocrat is sole legislator.

With the third century of our era the great constructive period of the Roman jurists came to an end, and with Diocletian there opened the era of codification. About this time (? 295) a collection of the constitutions issued by the Emperors from Hadrian to Diocletian was made by a certain Gregorius, who may have been a professor at the great law school of Beirut in Syria, and not much later a compilation of the constitutions of Diocletian was made by one Hermogenianus, which served as a supplement to the work of Gregorius. Theodosius II in 429 would seem to have conceived the idea of making a general code which should contain a statement of the whole of the current law, and should take the place of all former legislation and jurisprudence. He would thus have anticipated the work of Justinian. The project, however, was dropped, we know not why; but a collection of imperial constitutions was compiled by commissioners appointed in 435, and was published early in 438. The Theodosian code came into force both in West and East in 439.

But the compilation of this new code did not bring with it any cessation of imperial legislation, and thus, as Justinian complained, obscurity and contradictions were introduced into the body of Roman Law : cases in the courts of justice tended to become interminably protracted, and judgments to be founded less on statutory provisions than on the arbitrary caprice of the judges.

It was the belief of Justinian that on an

Emperor of Rome was laid a double task : he must be at once the military conqueror, and the supreme legislator. If the eternal city had grown great through the triumph of her arms and the justice of her laws, it was his duty as heir of Rome's past to be worthy of his two-fold heritage. Under his direction there should be a great stock-taking of the law of Rome.

In his minister of justice (quæstor of the Sacred Palace) Tribonian, a native of Pamphylia, the Emperor found a man after his own heart, whose prodigious learning and zeal Justianian is never tired of celebrating. In April 529 a new code was issued based on the Gregorian, Hermogenian and Theodosian codes, but containing the constitutions of later Emperors which were still in force. The work was carried through post haste : the ten commissioners had needed but little more than a year for its completion.

But it was in the *Digest* that Justinian's real originality was shown. The sixteen new commissioners appointed in December 530 were to make a selection from the works of the great jurists which should not only be of service to the practitioner by the removal of repetitions and contradictions and by the omission of discussions on matters which had now become obsolete, but which should preserve the memorials of Rome's great jurists from oblivion, and should incite the present generation to their study. The colossal task of reading and extracting 2,000 books, containing about 3,000,000 lines, seemed to

G

Justinian himself all but an impossibility, only to be attempted with the aid of God : ten years were thought to be necessary for its completion : in fact it was achieved in three; in December 533 the Digest was promulgated, and thus in 150,000 lines was reared in the Emperor's phrase " a holy temple of Roman justice."

This selection from the works of the Roman jurists superseded the originals, and when we consider the brief space of time in which the Digest was compiled, it is only natural that there should be much imperfection in the composition; the system of arrangement of the extracts is often superficial; worse still, urge the critics, the ancient texts are abbreviated, mutilated, cut into dispersed fragments, like the body of Medea's child, and worst of all interpolated by the hand of a vandal innovator. Tribonian and his accomplices, it has been well said, have been treated by modern students more as slaves who have plundered their master's treasures than as guardians who have saved what was possible from a general conflagration. But the critic must not forget that within the Roman Empire constructive juristic talent had disappeared : the use of the works of the classical jurists by the judges under Valentinian's law of Citations of 476 had sunk to the arithmetical labour of counting heads, so that the mere number of authorities adduced by an advocate carried the day. Already in the West editorial scissors had begun to snip elaborate treatises into con-

venient lengths, and when we survey the
succession of late Byzantine manuals, growing
ever more meagre and less scientific, we may
well doubt whether even in the East the
Empire would have preserved works for which
it had lost a true understanding.   Further it
must be remembered that Justinian's aim was
not purely scientific, but also practical : he
sought to issue a code of present law to meet
the needs of the men of his own time : his
Corpus Juris Civilis was to be a guide to judges,
a manual for teachers, and a fount of justice
for his subjects; and here other critics have
complained that he was too timid a revolu-
tionary : that he lacked the courage boldly
to break with tradition, and left it to the
Iconoclasts to carry his own legal reforms to
their logical conclusion.   Indeed the greatness
of Justinian as a legislator surely lies in this :
realising that a nation's law is an organic
development resuming in itself a people's
history, despite his desire to simplify Roman
procedure and to introduce greater humanity
into the administration of Roman justice, he
yet did not produce merely a practical manual,
but something greater, a work which, to use
his own figure, might serve as a citadel behind
whose walls the treasures of the past could be
safeguarded from the assaults of envious time
and which in due course was to reveal to the
nations of the barbarous West the idea of a
state based upon a foundation of law.

But the law thus codified was to be no dead
letter : it must be accessible to new genera-

tions of students. For their use was issued
in November 533 an introduction to Roman
Law—the *Institutes*—moulded on an earlier
manual of the jurist Gaius, but containing
those changes in the law which had resulted
from the later imperial legislation. The code
of 530 was superseded in 534 by the New Code,
and it is the text of this later version that has
survived. The Emperor's work was complete:
he saw that it was good.

We still possess nearly 600 of Justinian's
constitutions; in every sphere his reforming
energy is manifested : the wife's rights were
extended, particularly with regard to her
dowry, while it was made obligatory upon the
husband to settle on the wife property equal
in value to that of her dowry; the child won
greater freedom both of person and property;
in future he could only be disinherited on
certain statutory grounds, and, if he were
disinherited, the parent must expressly state
the ground for disherison; the slave was safeguarded from the cruelty of his master, and
could claim the protection of the magistrate;
the law of succession was entirely remodelled
and based throughout on blood relationship,
while obsolete forms which time had rendered
largely meaningless were.abolished in the case
of adoption, manumission, land-transfer and
other transactions. " Humanity," natural
reason and public utility were the principles
by which the Emperor himself claimed to have
been guided in his reforms.

Justinian issued the great body of his legislation in the Latin tongue, the tongue of the West : it was published when he was about to take in hand the recovery of the West for the Empire. Himself sprung from the Latin-speaking Danube lands, in this act he expresses his loyalty to the proud Roman tradition of world rule. But, while this is true, the Latin cause at Constantinople was already lost. The Emperor was legislating in a Greek city. Upon his commission of lawyers no western university is represented, not a single member is drawn from the older Rome; many of his innovations are derived from Hellenistic sources, while the new constitutions (*Novels*) which Justinian promulgated after 534 are themselves written in the Greek tongue.

During the latter part of the sixth century Justinian's veto on the composition of further works upon his new legislation—whether commentaries or paraphrases—was disregarded, and a considerable legal literature in the Greek language was produced, of which unfortunately but little has been preserved. Though the Emperors of the seventh century issued constitutions from time to time, these mainly concerned public administration, or the relation of church and state. It was only with the Iconoclast Emperors that widespread changes were made in the private law. In 739 the *Écloga* was promulgated, *i.e.* a selection of laws taken from the legislation of Justinian with modifications " in the direction of greater humanity." But these developments were for the most part reversed and abolished by

Basil the Macedonian, who returned once more to the law of the sixth century. Some time between 870–879 a new manual—*Procheiron*—was officially promulgated to take the place of the Ecloga, while a commission was appointed to prepare a full code from which should be banished the perversions of the laws introduced by the heretic Image-breakers. Between 879–886 an improved hand-book—the *Epanagoge*—was compiled, but probably never received official sanction. Whether the larger compilation of Basil in 40 books was ever published is doubtful: certain it is that we possess only, and that not completely, the code promulgated by his successor Leo VI—the *Basilika* (or imperial ordinances) in sixty books. Even after the publication of the Basilika the works of Justinian were still studied, especially in the eleventh century, when in 1045 Constantine Monomachus established a law school in Constantinople under Johannes Xiphilinus. It has been thought that this revival of legal studies had considerable influence on the study of the law of Justinian in eleventh-century Bologna : but this hypothesis is very doubtful, and the activity of the new Byzantine school was probably, as we saw (p. 163), short-lived. At the end of the twelfth century the view gained ground that the Basilika alone represented living law, and in the decay of legal science the development of Roman private law after the reign of Leo VI came to a standstill. There follows a period of manuals and compendia :

the Basilika were neglected, and the decline culminated in the *Hexabiblos* of Harmenopoulos, produced about 1345—" a miserable epitome of the epitomes of epitomes." Byzantine law in its last days had become in Mr. Ashburner's phrase " an ungodly jumble."

Scholars have attributed to the Iconoclast Emperors the promulgation of three small codes, the Farmer's Law, The Soldier's Law and The Sailor's Law. But this view is now generally abandoned. Mr. Ashburner has, for example, made it probable that the Sailor's Law was put together by a private hand between A.D. 600 and A.D. 800, and that it was compiled from material of very different epochs and characters. Some of it was possibly from treatises in the nature of a " Complete Merchant," guides to a gentleman engaging in business; other parts may come from enactments of Byzantine Cæsars, but the mass of it must be derived from local customs. Panchenko in the same way has shown that the Farmer's Law is a compilation of village custom serving to supplement the general imperial law, and dating from a similar period (see ch. vi), while the Soldier's Law is largely a paraphrase of passages in Justinian's Digest and Code. None of these codes has any demonstrable connection with the Iconoclast Emperors.

It remains to suggest in outline what were some of the principal influences which affected the development of later Roman law prior to the period of decay. These may be roughly distinguished as (i) the influence of general Christian sentiment, (ii) the influence of the Church as an organisation, often expressing its will through councils and synods by means of canons, and (iii) popular custom, especially of the eastern provinces. Naturally these are constantly overlapping, and in any particular case it may be difficult to say which has been the predominant influence. A few examples must suffice.

(i) It was naturally only after the conversion of Constantine that Christian sentiment could influence imperial legislation; Christian sentiment, it is true, never sought to remodel the private law of the Roman Empire (cf. p. 241), but from the fourth century onwards its power steadily increased. It is seen in the civil disabilities imposed upon heretics, in the legitimation by a subsequent marriage of children born of a concubine, and also in a new method of manumitting slaves in the face of the church. More remarkable was the removal of the penalties against celibacy, and the grant of civil jurisdiction to bishops, if both (or one only?) of the parties so desired. The Christian conception of marriage as an identification of husband and wife so that they become one flesh—a relation which excludes all sexual intercourse with any third person—was not carried to its logical conclusion by Justinian : he still recognised concubinage, and in consequence legitimation. It was left for the Iconoclast Emperors to refuse to admit any connection save that of mono-

gamous marriage, while corporal and pecuniary
punishments were introduced by them for any
connection other than that of wedlock. Re-
marriage was unrestricted under the law of
Justinian : but the Empress Irene forbad a
third or any further marriage; even the
Macedonian Emperors, though reintroducing a
recognition of concubinage, treated a fourth
marriage as null and void, while a third
remained subject to the ecclesiastical penalties
of the canon law. Divorce was permitted on
many grounds by Justinian despite the Christian conception of marriage, only divorce by
mutual consent being prohibited. The Iconoclast Emperors sought to limit the number of
grounds for divorce to four, among which were
leprosy or attempts by husband or wife on each
other's life (but not insanity); the Macedonian
Emperors restored the law as it had been
under Justinian. On the subject of divorce
Church and State never came to an agreement.

The most interesting features of the Iconoclast legislation are connected with family
relations, and at the foundation of these provisions rests the Christian view of the family
as a unity bound together by ties of loving
interdependence : the relation, for example, of
the wife to her husband is no longer that of
subjection under her husband's authority
(*manus*), as in the early Roman marriage, nor
of independence, as in the later " free marriage,"
but rights and property are enjoyed by husband and wife in community. The attitude

of the State to the children becomes one of
fatherly interest and of concern in their
welfare : it stands as protector of their rights.
Thus the Ecloga gives to the wife new powers
and privileges. It places the mother, so far
as the *person* of her child is concerned, on the
same footing as the father; her consent to the
child's marriage as well as that of her husband
must be secured, and, if she survive her
husband, she can now appoint by will a
guardian for her child to act after her death—
a right only recently acquired by married
women in this country (Guardianship of
Infants Act, 1888). The Ecloga further established a *community* in the settled property of
husband and wife, where Justinian had rested
content with the mathematical idea of a
necessary *equality* in the value of the property
which each spouse brought into settlement,
though it is true that such community may
only last during the joint lives of husband and
wife, the property of each reverting, on the
death of the other without issue, to his or her
representatives.

With respect to the children of the marriage
the old absolute power over their life and
property which belonged to the head of the
family had long broken down : the jurisdiction of the family tribunal had passed to the
representative of the State, the child's gains
were in general, since the time of Justinian, his
own property. Emancipation of children from
the *patria potestas* (the absolute power of the
head of the family over all its members) could

now probably be effected at the will either of
the child or parent; and by virtue of the
legislation of the Iconoclasts on the death
of one parent while a child was a minor the
surviving parent was bound to administer the
whole of the common property of husband and
wife for the children's benefit, and a child
could not be disinherited by his parent unless
a judicial authority determined that the
child by its misconduct had forfeited the right
to a share in the parental estate. If no guardian was nominated by the will of the surviving parent, the public orphanage or one of the
churches in Constantinople—in the provinces
a bishop or a monastery—was appointed to
act as such guardian. Finally, through the
Christian view that parents owed an equal love
to all children, it was felt that here too equity
loves equality, and that the parent's property
should be equally divided amongst the
children. Thus family settlements with un-
equal division according to the varying
circumstances of the children's position were
never favoured in later Roman law.

It is true that most of these provisions were
abrogated by the Macedonian Emperors; but
it is probable that in customary usage much
of the Iconoclast legislation remained in force.

(ii) The influence of the Church can in many
cases hardly be distinguished from that of
general Christian sentiment. It is seen, for
example, in the laws on the subject of marriage,
to which reference has already been made,
where canons of church councils often formed

the model for imperial constitutions : this is especially true of the successive narrowing of the sphere of relationship within which marriages could be contracted. Thus relationship among collaterals up to the seventh degree became a bar to marriage, relationship arising from adoption was ultimately held to have the same effect in this respect as blood relationship, while even the fact of godparentage was held to create an impediment to marriage in certain cases. So far as the forms of marriage were concerned, the demand of the church that there should of necessity be a public ecclesiastical ceremony ultimately prevailed. The influence of the clergy may also be seen in the favour shown by the law to legacies for pious uses; Nicephorus Phocas failed in his attempt to stay the posthumous prodigality of his subjects in founding monasteries, while under Constantine Porphyrogenitus it was enacted that in the case of a subject dying childless and intestate one third of his estate should pass to the Church for the benefit of the soul of the deceased. Such instances could easily be multiplied, but these may suffice.

(iii) It is probable that even where no direct evidence can at present be adduced, many of the innovations introduced into Roman law by the Iconoclasts are in substance only a recognition of popular custom. Thus the essentially Roman idea of the *patria potestas* had never been understood by the Greek citizens of Asia, and must in practice have been largely disregarded : this tendency is reflected in the provisions of the Ecloga. The custom that a daughter who had received her dower should not inherit from her parents with her brothers and sisters would seem to have persisted even in the face of the express provision of the Basilika to the contrary effect, while the Syro-Roman law-book appears to have remained in force long after Justinian's legislation, although the latter was intended to supersede all other codes. Custom regarded writing as an essential of a valid contract and not merely as a means of proof of the terms of that contract, and this view had a marked effect in later Byzantine legislation; when it was enacted that, as a general rule, for an agreement to be enforceable at law either the document embodying the terms of that agreement must bear the sign of the Cross inscribed thereon by the party's own hand, or must contain an express invocation of the Holy Trinity, or otherwise the contract must be supported by the evidence of seven witnesses, it would seem that once more these provisions had their origin in popular usage. The executor of a Byzantine will—a person unknown to Roman practice—probably sprang from popular mistrust of the integrity of the heir-at-law.

In fact, we are only slowly realising through a closer study of the papyri that the unity and universality of Roman law and its enforcement throughout the Empire were, it is true, imperial ideals, but ideals which in practice fell far short of their full realisation. As yet we can only dimly discern those forces of inherited use and wont which reacted against the efforts of the capital to impose on all subjects alike one law, the will of the imperial successors of Constantine.

CHAPTER XIII

TRADE

The Roman Empire hath many privileges in that it is the first of Empires, and that it first believed in Christ, and that it doth service to every branch of the Christian economy : and there is yet another sign of the power which God hath accorded to the Romans, to wit, that it is with their coinage that all nations do their trade; it is received everywhere from one end of the earth to the other : it is admired by all men and every kingdom, for no other kingdom hath its like.—COSMAS (retired India Merchant who became a monk), *Topographia Christ.*, p. 148.

In the early Empire, as we have seen, it was the trade with the East which was of the first importance for Italy, for from the East were borne the luxuries, which had gradually come to be regarded as the necessities, of the West. The exports from Europe were quite insufficient to pay for the imports from Asia, and in the time of Pliny (*Hist. Nat.* xii. 41) specie to the amount of £800,000 was annually drained from the West to make good the debit balance of the account. When the capital had been moved to the Golden Horn, it was still the trade with the East that absorbed the best energies of the Roman merchants; the State in its turn was interested in this trade, for the

treasures of India and China judiciously
bestowed upon barbarian princes of the West
might serve to maintain the Empire's prestige
even where Roman arms had proved unsuccessful.   The power that held the storied East
in fee possessed a magic before which the rude
warrior chieftains of the invading hosts bowed
in awe.

There were three possible routes by which
the products of Further Asia might reach the
Roman merchant : the shortest was by the
oases of Sogdiana (Samarcand, Bokhara)
through Persia and thus to the frontier of the
Empire; the second through the Indian Ocean
up the Red Sea; the third, a much more difficult route, from Central Asia to the Caspian
and thence, avoiding Persian territory, to the
Black Sea.   With the growth of luxury the
demand for silk was ever on the increase.   In
private life robes of pure silk were now
common : the Church too, which had originally
refused to employ silk for ecclesiastical purposes, welcomed gifts of this precious material
for vestments, for hangings and draperies, and
for the adornment of its altars, while the
manufacture of certain forms of silk robes
used in court ceremonies was a monopoly of the
State.   For the supply of the new material,
however, the Empire was dependent upon the
caravans which traversed Persia, and in consequence the raw silk was liable to heavy
customs duties before the frontier was crossed.
Thus in the treaties between Persia and Rome
certain towns were specified through which

alone the raw silk could pass—Callinicum in
the south in Osroene, Nisibis in Mesopotamia
in the centre of the boundary line, Artaxata
and Dovin in Armenia on the north. As a
natural result of the frequent wars between
Byzantium and Persia Roman commerce
suffered heavily both through the interrup-
tion of communications and through the raising
of the price of the raw material. Since the
fifth century the State had intervened, and in
order to abolish competition only imperial
agents were allowed to purchase the silk at
the frontier, which was afterwards supplied to
private individuals at the price then current.
In the reign of Justinian the war with Persia
caused the price of raw material, and thus the
prices charged for the finished article by the
merchants of Tyre and Berytus, to rise to an
abnormal height. The Emperor accordingly
ordered that no silk should be bought at a
higher rate than that of 15 gold solidi for the
pound : but the only result of this edict was
that Persian merchants refused to sell their
merchandise at all, and thus the manufacturers
were ruined and the trade brought to a standstill. In face of this disaster the State was
forced to yield to the demands of the Persian
middlemen, but the entire manufacture became
a monopoly of the Roman State. Soon afterwards, however (between 552 and 554), two
monks from Serinda (? Khotan) or, as
Theophanes of Byzantium says, a Persian
monk from China—presumably a Nestorian
missionary—escaped the vigilance of the

Persians, and brought cocoons of the silk-worm to Justinian. Mulberry trees were planted in Syria, and the Empire began to produce its own silk; though for some time after the conclusion of peace the former traffic in silk through Persia was resumed, Rome had, in fact, become independent of the foreign market. The manufacture of silk remained an anxiously guarded imperial monopoly, employing thousands of workmen. It was only in the middle of the twelfth century when Roger II, the Norman ruler of Sicily, captured Thebes and Corinth and transported to Palermo the silk operatives from the factories of Greece that the Empire's secret was disclosed to the peoples of the West.

Justin II in the latter half of the sixth century endeavoured to open up the northern trade route, and with this object entered into negotiations with the Turkish Chagan, but the wars in the West distracted the Emperor's attention, and the project was allowed to drop. The ports, however, of the Crimea—Bosporos and Cherson—traded with the Huns and Avars of South Russia, and brought jewels and rich fabrics of Roman manufacture to be exchanged for the skins and slaves of the North, while for corn and salt and wine Caucasian tribesmen sold leather and furs.

Far more important was the Southern trade route of which we have an excellent account in the work of Cosmas Indicopleustes, who gives us his own experience as a merchant before he finally quitted worldly things in order to convince an incredulous generation that the world was indeed not round, as men impiously asserted. Ceylon, he tells us, was in the sixth century the meeting place for the merchants of the nearer and further East : traders from India and Ethiopia here exchanged the silk, aloes and sandal wood of China for the glass and embroideries of Syria; here were bartered the amber and jade of the West, the pepper of Malabar and the sesame wood and copper of Kalliana (near Bombay)— another great trade centre.

Axumite merchants brought these products to Adule on the Red Sea, the capital of the Ethiopian Kingdom of Axum. Some would sail as far as Ceylon, while the majority would seem to have laden their vessels at Malabar, whither Indian traders would bring the merchandise of the further east together with the pearls, sapphires and tortoise shells of Ceylon. The Axumite ships no longer hugged the land ; the regularity of the monsoons had been known since the reign of Vespasian, and making use of these the traders boldly struck out into the Indian Ocean.

Every other year, too, an expedition left Axum for the interior of Africa; in this many traders would join, so that the whole company would number some 500 men, and would thus be able to offer resistance to the attacks of hostile tribes. They carried with them cattle, iron and salt : on reaching their destination the cattle were slain and a thick thorn breastwork raised. On this the merchants placed their wares, and retired : the natives advanced, and would place on each a piece of gold in the shape of a bean, and then retreat. The traders in turn came forward, and, if satisfied, took the gift, when the native carried off the iron or salt : if dissatisfied, the gold remained untouched, and the native then added further gold, or, if he were not content to offer more, removed the precious metal. After four or five days the barter was ended, and the expedition returned with all speed to avoid the winter rains which made the river fords impassable. The journey there and back lasted six months. Who these barbarians with their beans of gold may have been is uncertain ; it has been suggested that the Axumite merchants may have penetrated to Zimbabwe, in which some explorers have thought to have found the Ophir of the Bible.

To Adule came the Roman ships, and thence sailed with cargoes of Eastern merchandise to Jotabe, an island off the end of the Sinaitic peninsula. At Jotabe would also arrive the Roman vessels trading in spices with the ports of Arabia Felix on the eastern coast of the Red Sea. Having paid their dues at the imperial customs station at Jotabe, they would either proceed up the western arm of the sea to Elath or else sail to Clysma (near Suez) whence a canal led to the Nile ; from Alexandria the produce of the East was distributed over the whole Mediterranean basin.

This Western trade was mainly in the hands of Syrians, and their influence only increased with the decline of the Roman civilisation through the invasions of the barbarians. From the fourth to the sixth centuries we have evidence of colonies of these Orientals, living as separate " nations " in the towns of the West, and in many cases retaining their own language. Coming for the most part as traders they naturally settled in the great commercial centres—in Italy, for example, at Naples and Ostia, in Gaul at Nice and Marseilles, then, as now, a meeting-place of East and West. Thus the river Garonne led them to Bordeaux, the Rhone and Saone to the north of Gaul through Vienne and Lyons, and the Loire to Orleans and Tours, while they can be traced even in England and Germany.

The reconquest of Africa by Justinian resulted in a wonderful revival of its prosperity : to the Arab invaders lands which are now a desert appeared a very garden of delight ; Justinian did all in his power to encourage the export trade of his eastern harbours with Africa and Italy. From Syria, then one of the most fertile countries in the world, came silk, the wines of Gaza, Sarepta and Ascalon, the glass of Sidon, elaborately worked stuffs from Tyre and Berytus, while Egypt sent papyrus and the spices which had come to her from the further East.

Even in the troubled years of the early seventh century, although Slav raiders had ventured on the open seas, trade between Africa and Constantinople continued, and Alexandrian ships penetrated as far as Britain.

Through the seventh and eighth centuries it was part of the imperial policy to foster Eastern influence in Italy, but in the ninth the two halves of the Mediterranean were almost completely severed—communication for example between Spain and the Eastern Empire ceased altogether.

But in the ninth and tenth centuries a new outlet for the products of the Empire was found in the trade with Russia (cf. ch. xiv). The Prince of Kiev would organise the expedition, carrying the tribute paid in kind which had been collected during the winter. The merchants of other neighbouring market-towns would take part in order to be safe-guarded from Chazar attacks by the military forces of Kiev. The voyage down the Dnieper was one of great danger and difficulty, for where the long series of rapids breaks the course of the stream the boats had at times to be drawn over land, while hostile tribesmen would choose this moment for their attacks. But the Black Sea once reached, the treaties between Kiev and Constantinople assured the traders admission within the walls of New Rome, provided that they entered by one gate only unarmed, and in parties of not more than fifty at a time : here they might stay for the summer, but no longer. The Russian merchants were accorded free board and " baths " by the Government during their visit, and special allowances were made to the official trading commissioners of the Prince of Kiev : no tolls were exacted from any of the Russian merchants. In return for these privileges the Russians covenanted to protect the territory of the Empire; thus, for instance, the Prince of Rus undertook not to permit the Bulgars of the Crimea to ravage the district of Cherson. Trade was conducted almost wholly by barter. Russian furs, honey, wax and slaves were exchanged for Greek wines, fruits and silk stuffs. On their return the merchants were given by the Roman Government provisions for the journey home, as well as such shipping tackle—anchors, cables, ropes and sails—as required to be made good. The reader should consult the brilliant account of this trade with the Empire which will be found in the first volume of Kluchevsky's *History of Russia*.

From the tenth century also dates the *Eparchikon Biblion*—or collection of regulations issued by the State for the trade guilds of Constantinople. This "Book of the Prefect of the City," the official who controlled with but few exceptions all the guilds of the capital so far as their relations towards the State were concerned, was only discovered in 1893: its value can hardly be over-estimated. The outstanding feature of its provisions is the protection accorded alike to consumer and producer; the State sets its ban upon forestalling as well as regrating: everything, so far as possible, is to be bought or sold without the intervention of the middleman, while provision is made to secure the workman his due wage, to check the avarice of the capitalist, and to prevent the monopolising of an industry by the wealthy few. All those employed in the principal trades are united in a guild, and no man must belong to two guilds at one and the same time. Where the State is especially interested, as in the question of food supply, the regulations to which the members of the guild are subject are peculiarly detailed : the State determines the price at which the raw materials are to be bought, and the price at which food is to be sold, and in several cases it would appear that the State can demand service from the guilds for which it makes no payment—a trace perhaps of the old Greek practice of *leitourgiai*, under which voluntary public services were imposed by the State upon its wealthy citizens. The appointment of the Presidents of the guilds was probably in every case dependent upon the approval of the Prefect of the City, while to facilitate state control all sales were to be public, and could generally only be made at stated places prescribed for each particular trade. The guild alone purchased materials which it then distributed amongst its members, and these purchases by the officials of the guilds can again be made only in specified localities. Violations of these regulations were punished with exclusion from the guild, confiscation of property, or money penalties, flogging and shaving off of the hair of head and beard, and in more serious cases with exile or loss of a hand. All foreign merchants on arriving in the capital were bound to report themselves to the State authorities; they could not stay in Constantinople more than three months, save under the terms of a special treaty, and if at the expiration of this period they had not sold their wares, the State would undertake the arrangements for their sale. All their purchases in the city itself are scrutinised, and they are not allowed to carry away articles which, like the finer kinds of silk stuffs, are forbidden to be exported. All merchandise is inspected, and then, if passed for export, is marked with the State seal.

But with the eleventh and twelfth century Byzantine commerce declined, for the failure of the State to maintain its navy forced the Empire to purchase the help of Venice by ruinous concessions. Venice, founded probably about the middle of the sixth century, still formed, in the eighth, part of the Italian domains of the Eastern Empire, but she developed an independent navy of her own which from the year 727 we find acting in support of the Byzantine exarch in Italy. The island city stepped into the place of Ravenna, when the capital of the exarchate fell to the Lombards in 751, and Constantinople in the early years of the ninth century vainly forbad the Venetian merchants to trade in ships, timber and war-material with the Mohammedan rulers of Egypt. In the tenth century correspondence between Constantinople and the West regularly passed through Venetian hands, while ambassadors from Germany travelled from Venice on Venetian ships, among others

the famous Bishop Liutprand of Cremona.
When in 991 the Empire concluded a commercial treaty with Venice, it was a clear sign
that the city was hardly any longer regarded
as a state subject to Rome. But the fatal
step was taken when Alexius I paid for
Venetian help against Robert Guiscard the
Norman by signing the treaty of the year 1082,
granting to merchants of Venice complete
freedom from tolls or duties throughout the
Empire, and a quarter in Constantinople on
the Golden Horn. John Comnenus might
withdraw these privileges, he might grant
lesser favours to Genoese and Pisans, and
attempt to weaken Venice by their rivalry,
but the effort was fruitless : the Roman navy
was no match for that of Venice; the Empire
was forced to restore her former privileges,
and it was Venetian craft which finally led
the Crusaders to attack Constantinople in the
Fourth Crusade. After the fall of the capital
the commerce of the Empire never regained
the ground which it had lost.

How is the decline of Roman commerce to
be explained ? Doubtless there were many
causes : it must suffice to mention one which
would seem to have played an important part.
The wealthy Roman was unwilling to hazard
his capital in over-sea commerce, but preferred to invest it in land. The risks were
indeed great : it was true that ships no longer
sailed in the winter, what had been in classical
times regulated by the *custom* of mariners was
now provided for by *law*. Statutes of Italian

towns enact generally that sailings must be
suspended from November 1 to March 1.
There were dangers from fire, dangers from
wreckers, dangers from land-robbers and
dangers from pirates. There was the danger of
reprisals when, as often happened, a state
would grant to its wronged subject the right
of avenging himself upon any ship of the state
whose citizen had inflicted the injury. There
was the peril of meeting corsairs, folk of
exemplary piety, who thus gained money to
go on pilgrimages in honour of Our Lady;
folk also of surprising freedom of speech :
when the Pisans in 1165, Mr. Ashburner tells
us, asked a distinguished Genoese corsair where
he was going, " I am going," was the answer,
" to capture you and your goods and persons,
and to cut off your noses." Thus ships went
generally in batches (mudue) to render each
other mutual support, and carried men at
arms on board. Now according to maritime
law if money were lent on a vessel and that
vessel were lost, the money lent could not be
recovered. The Roman of the later Empire
was not content to take this risk : he invested
in land, and then by his will left that land as a
provision for his soul to a monastery : the
Venetian made his charitable donations in
money with directions that the capital should
be employed in trade. The struggle between
Constantinople and Venice is the struggle
between a territorial and a commercial
aristocracy, a struggle which has been
repeated in our own time, and it was the

tragedy of the Empire that the investors who played for safety lost the day.

But that coinage which Cosmas had praised outlived the commerce of Constantinople; and far into the later Middle Ages the besants of New Rome had free course in East and West alike.

CHAPTER XIV

THE DEBT OF THE SLAVS TO BYZANTIUM

A people of inheritance, as ye are this day.—Deut. iv. 20.

IT was from Constantinople, probably in the year A.D. 864, that Constantine or, to give him his later ecclesiastical name, Cyril, set forth with his brother Methodius on a mission to the Slavs of Moravia in answer, as tradition asserts, to the request of their Prince Rostislav that some one might be sent to teach them the whole truth. Before this date we have no evidence that the Slavs possessed any literature of their own, or, indeed, that they employed any written characters which could form a medium for literary expression. Constantine had formerly acted as an imperial governor in Macedonia, and had there learned the Slav tongue; he it was who invented a new script, derived ultimately from Greek minuscule characters, and translated parts of the New Testament and probably a lectionary into the dialect of the Macedonian Slavs; these translations he carried with him to Moravia, though whether they were not originally intended for Christian propaganda in Bulgaria may here be left an open question.

This new script used in the Moravian Mission was the so-called Glagolitic, or old Church Slavonic: that Cyril also invented the alphabet which bears his name—the " Cyrillic "—based on Greek uncial writing and now used by Russians, Serbians and Bulgarians we can neither positively assert nor deny, but it seems probable that this simple script was the product of a later age.[1] For three years the brothers worked together in Moravia, but in A.D. 867 they carried to Rome the body of S. Clement which Cyril had miraculously discovered some years before and brought back from Cherson after a missionary journey to the land of the Chazars. It was important to secure Rome's approval of the use of a liturgy in the Slav tongue, for it was thought that only in the three languages—Hebrew, Greek and Latin—which had been used in the superscription on the Cross of Christ could Christian worship be duly celebrated. Rome for the time adopted a liberal view, and authorised the use of a Slavonic service-book, but after Cyril's death (869), although Methodius returned to his mission field, the Roman clergy finally triumphed, and the national language (save for a few exceptions) was forbidden in the liturgy of those Slavs who were dependent on the Roman Church. The Moravian Mission was thus ultimately unsuccessful, but to-day all Slavs, whether they profess allegiance to

[1] For a comparison of these scripts see the table given by Dr. Minns in his article " Slavs," *Encyclopædia Britannica*, vol. xxv. p. 232.

the Western or the Eastern Church, claim as a common heritage the glory of the two great missionaries sent to them by Photius the Patriarch of Constantinople. In this chapter we are to attempt very briefly to characterise the debt of Bulgar, Serb and Russian to the civilisation of East Rome.

(i) The Finno-Turkish Bulgars on their settlement in the Danube lands were early influenced by their Slav subjects, and adopted the Slav language. During the course of the seventh century the sons of Kubrat founded the first Bulgarian Kingdom with its capital, recently excavated by Russian archæologists, at Aboba. But the royal power was weakened by the feuds of the boyards, and it was only in the ninth century under the great warrior Krum (802–815) and his successor Omortag (815–830?) that Bulgaria was reunited. To Omortag is due the foundation of the new capital at Preslav. Boris (852–888) deserted the faith of his fathers and adopted Christianity. The great question on which the future history of his kingdom depended was therefore one of ecclesiastical allegiance : Rome and Constantinople both claimed the royal convert. Boris, however, failed to obtain from the Pope the consecration of Formosus as Bulgarian bishop or patriarch, and was in consequence thrown into the arms of the Orthodox Church. At a council held in 870 A.D. the Eastern clergy, supported by Basil I, determined that since the territories of Bulgaria had once formed part of the

Eastern Empire, the Bulgarian Church should naturally depend upon the patriarch of Constantinople. Boris had begun his reign by conquering further territory on his Western frontiers : after his conversion Bulgaria, instead of turning to the reduction of the Serbs and the Slavs of Croatia, fell under the spell of East Rome. " The Bulgarian Kings had it in their power to found a great Slav Empire : they despised it and dreamed only of supplanting the Empire of Byzantium." Set between the Christian Frank of the West and the Christian Roman of the East, Boris made his momentous choice, and despite negotiations with the Papacy entered into from time to time for passing political ends, Bulgaria has never wavered in her allegiance to the Orthodox Church.

Although the Christianity of Boris might savour rather of the steppe than of the gospel, his successor Simeon the Great (893–927) was " half a Greek," and through his education in Constantinople " the new Ptolemy " was master of all the learning of his day. Student of the philosophy of Aristotle, he was yet a redoubtable warrior, and after his defeat of the Empire's forces at Anchialos in 917 he assumed the proud title of " Emperor and Autocrator of all the Bulgarians and Greeks." But during the long period of peace between Bulgaria and East Rome which preceded the breach of 913, the Court of Preslav had been reconstructed on the Byzantine model. The northward expansion of Bulgaria was barred by the

Patzinaks; the settlement of the Hungarians on Save and Danube drove a wedge between the Eastern and the Western Slavs, and cut off Moravia and Carinthia. Bulgaria, limited to the Balkan peninsula, was driven to closer relations with East Rome. Palaces and churches were built and filled with paintings, with marble, silver and gold. The King on his throne, girt with purple and arrayed in pearl-embroidered robes, was surrounded by a dazzling suite of boyards. " If a stranger returning from Preslav," wrote John the Exarch, " were asked what he had seen there he could only reply, ' I do not know how to describe it all; your own eyes alone could give you an idea of such splendour.' "

On the accession of Simeon's son Peter (927–969), who married a Byzantine princess, peace was concluded with East Rome, while in 945 Constantinople consented to recognise the independent Patriarchate of Bulgaria, and to accord to Peter the long-coveted title of Emperor. Under the patronage of Simeon and his son a Bulgarian literature was created; a sort of academy was formed under the leadership of Clement, subsequently created Metropolitan of Bulgaria, and among the scholars who rendered accessible to the young Slav Church the treasures of Greek theology the most famous names are those of Constantine, of the monk Hrabr and of John the Exarch. This literature is a literature of translations, and since the clergy were its authors, it was in the main an ecclesiastical

H

literature; it consisted of such works as the
sermons of Chrysostom, the discourses of
Athanasius, the theological treatises of John
of Damascus; history was represented by a
version of the chronicle of John Malalas, while
the Sbornik of Simeon was a general encyclopædia of the Byzantine knowledge of the time.
It was a prose literature and like its Greek
originals it was often rhetorical; adopting
foreign and oriental themes—stories from the
Arabian Nights, the legends of Troy and of
Alexander the Great,—it remained an exotic
product : Bulgaria has no annals such as the
Ancient Russian Chronicle which commonly
passes under the name of the Chronicle of
Nestor. Even the Puritan sectaries, such as
the Bogomils, derived the apocryphal works
which they disseminated from popular Greek
treatises. At this time, too, versions were
probably made of Byzantine legal codes, such
as the Ecloga and the Procheiron, while legal
compilations from Byzantine and Hebrew
sources were also produced. Thus Roman
conceptions made their way into the customary law of the Southern Slavs : the sole
responsibility of the wrongdoer, for example,
takes the place of the responsibility of the
family.

The Empire of Eastern Bulgaria fell as a
result of the victories of Nicephorus Phocas
and John Zimisces (963–972), and the conquests of the Shishmanids of Western Bulgaria
only led to the terrible campaigns of Basil II,
which destroyed the independence of the

Bulgarian State. Greek-speaking clergy occupied the principal sees of Bulgaria, and Slav literature declined; even when John and Peter Asen founded the later Bulgarian Empire at Trnovo (1186–1258) there was no second Simeon to herald a literary renascence; it was only in the fourteenth century that literature revived, the greatest representative of this mid-Bulgarian period being Euthymy, the last Patriarch of Trnovo (elected c. 1375). Translations from the Greek were once more predominant. Indeed in the restored Bulgarian Empire Byzantine influence was everywhere in the ascendant; communication between the two states was frequent : as Constantinople was the secular and religious centre for the Roman Empire, so round Trnovo, the Bulgarian capital, were gathered the monasteries, and in Trnovo were guarded the relics which inspired the lives of the saints composed by Euthymy. Bulgaria remained a reflex of New Rome, the land in which the thought and civilisation of Byzantium were more potent than in any other Slavonic country.

" The age of Simeon," writes Professor Sigel of Warsaw, " had an extraordinary importance for the whole of the Slavonic orthodox world. Here Greek literature . . . was made for the first time accessible to the Slavs; here the literary riches were accumulated which fostered for centuries the life of Serbia, Roumania and Russia."

(ii) It is only during the period of Serbian

national expansion under the dynasty founded
by Stefan Nemanya (Great Zupan ca. 1171–
1195 : died as the monk Simeon on Mount
Athos 1200) that our information as to the
life of the people and the organisation of the
Serbian state is at all satisfactory. The new
dynasty extended its authority from its centre
in Novi-Pazar; Stefan, at first a vassal of
Manuel I Comnenus, became fully independent
only after the latter's death in 1180. Stefan's
son, Stefan the First-crowned, received his
crown from the Papal legate in 1217, but this
dependence on Rome was short-lived; the
life-work of Namanya and his sons was in fact
to establish in their Kingdom the supremacy
of Byzantine civilisation and of the Eastern
Church. The growth of the Serbian realm
only began towards the end of the thirteenth
century : Stefan Urosh II (Milutin) won for
Serbia the leading position among the states
of the Balkan peninsula : Stefan Urosh III
conquered Bulgarian territory, and ruled over
North Macedonia, until at length Stefan Dushan
the Strong (1331–1335) subdued the whole of
Macedonia as far as Thessalonica, extending
his authority over Albania, Thessaly, Epirus
and Acarnania. In Skopje (Usküb) he was
crowned (1346) Czar of the Romaioi and
Serbians, while the bishop of Pec (Ipek) was
created Patriarch alike of Serbians and
Greeks. With his son Urosh ended the dynasty
(died 1371), and the glory of the Serbian state
was destroyed by the Turks in the terrible
battle of Kosovo-polje (1389), where the

Serbian Prince Lazar fell, though literary activity in Serbia reached its height in the reign of Despot Stefan Lazarevic (1389–1427). After the battle of Varna (1444) and the fall of Constantinople, Serbia became a Turkish province in 1459.

Just as Serbia's foreign policy mainly consisted in its relations with the restored Byzantine Empire, so throughout the history of the Kingdom the influence of Constantinople was paramount; but inasmuch as Serbian territory included a large stretch of the Adriatic coastline (extending from the mouth of the Drin to the north of the Narenta, excluding the lands of the republic of Ragusa), the way was also open for communication with the West. There were thus large numbers of Westerners settled in the country, as merchants, miners or foreign mercenaries, while constant relations were maintained with Venice and Ragusa.

Just as the chapel of S. Stephen was often chosen for Byzantine coronations (stephanos = a crown), so Stephen—the name taken by all the Kings of the dynasty of the Nemanjici— was the patron saint of the state. The monarch rules by divine right, and the Byzantine imperial formulæ and titles are rendered word for word in the usage of the Serbian Court. The administrative hierarchy was formed after the model of East Rome, even the tax-collector was known as " phrahtor " (= Grk. praktor). As the Roman chancery had two branches, one for Greek, the other for Latin correspondence, so the Serbian chancery corresponded with East Rome in the Greek tongue, and with the West in Latin. Imperial documents bore Byzantine names, and Byzantine diplomatic practice was followed. The divisions of the Serbian army were based on a decimal system after the Byzantine model, and soldiers were granted lands for their support, just as in the military organisation of East Rome (the system of Proniya is known in Serbia since 1300, though the date of its introduction is uncertain). Even the Zadruga—the custom for several generations to live together in one extensive homestead—has been traced by Peisker to the influence of the Byzantine hearth-tax (*kapnikon*) which favoured the growth of such large families. In ecclesiastical matters the dependence upon the Eastern Empire is even more striking. The golden age of Serbian architecture (1280–1360) marked the triumph of Byzantine influence; the churches were modelled on those of Thessalonica and of the Athos monasteries. The absence of statuary and the presence of icons painted on wood and covered with gold and silver only afford further evidence of East Roman inspiration. Monasteries grew apace, and with them the passion for retirement from a sinful world. Roman Catholicism was repressed, and Bogomilism extirpated. Serbian literature—the child of the monastery, and especially of the monastery of Chilandar on Mount Athos—was throughout dependent upon Byzantium; works on mysticism and asceticism—the monk's study—take the first

place. Adapting to its own use Bulgarian
translations, both of the age of Simeon and
also of the mid-Bulgarian period, its characteristics are similar to those of the earlier literature, though here, as Strzygowski has shown,
there was also direct contact with the Near
East, especially with Syria, Palestine and the
monastery on Sinai. The miniatures of the
fifteenth-century Serbian psalter in the Munich
library are copied from a Syrian original.
Through these translations of foreign works
the Serbs developed the language which was
to flower in those epics of the struggle with
the Turk which are Serbia's national glory
to-day. Even the legal code of the Tsar Dushan
was probably inspired by its author's desire to
emulate the Byzantine Emperors, while in the
life of the people the Serbian spring festival,
when the young folk went dancing through
the villages, preserved in its name—the
Rusalia—the memory of the Byzantine
" festival of roses " (Rosalia).

But the debtor seldom loves his creditor :
the Serbians disliked the eunuchs of Byzantium; the " slimness " of the Greek—his
astutia—was proverbial, and in the popular
story of the talking animals he is represented
by the fox. The Greek in his turn scoffed at
the imitation of Byzantine pomp and circum-
stance which he found at the Serbian Court :
" apes act in apeish wise, men say," was the
comment of Nicephorus Gregoras. To the
Byzantine the Serbian was for the most part a
brigand or a cattle-lifter, and more than one

writer laments the lot of an ambassador to
Serbia.   But though late in Serbia's history
political differences may have produced mutual
ill-will, this could not lessen Serbia's immense
debt to East Rome.

(iii) Though it may sound a paradox, the
assertion that the early Russian State owed its
very existence to Constantinople would hardly
be an exaggeration.   For when the Varan-
gians from the Scandinavian lands passed
from Novgorod to Kiev, it was here that the
Russia of history had its birth; and the
importance of Kiev lay in the fact that it
controlled the river basin of the Dnieper, and
therefore the highway which led to the Black
Sea and Byzantium.   But between Kiev and
the Black Sea lay the realm of the Chazars and
later of the Patzinaks.   To defend their commerce the princes of Kiev needed a military
force; the possession of this military force led
to the adhesion of other Russian provinces
formed about a market town as their centre :
to safeguard their trade interests merchants
sought the protection of the convoys of Kiev,
and thus contributed to extend the authority
of its Varangian prince.   In fact the whole economic life of the young state depended on its
trade with the Eastern Empire; in the winter
the princes collected their tribute in kind, and
in the spring this tribute formed the merchandise with which the ships for Constantinople
were laden, while in the forests higher up the
river the building of these ships furnished their
livelihood to the woodmen.   The wars and

treaties of Kiev with East Rome were generally commercial wars and commercial treaties, their object being to force the Romans to receive Russian traders and Russian merchandise. Vasilievsky has shown that already in the early years of the ninth century Russian ships were sailing in the Black Sea.

It is to Constantinople also that Russia owes her Christianity. The conversion of the Princess Olga in 957 might appear to have borne little fruit, but when Vladimir after his capture of Cherson in 988 received baptism in the Church of the Panagia—the all-holy Mother of God—in that city, and married the Byzantine princess Anna, he imposed his new faith on his pagan subjects and Kiev became a Christian state, and an ally of the Empire. The conversion of the powerful lord of Kiev is indeed one of the outstanding events in world history.

Christianity was introduced into Russia as a system already formed : the Russian Church was thus a copy of the Byzantine Church, its whole internal and external ecclesiastical life was moulded from Constantinople. Thus was determined the character of its dogma, its worship, its discipline : thence it drew its constitution and its law. The Russian Church was under a single Metropolitan, who was appointed by the Patriarch of Constantinople, and was usually a Greek; the Patriarch could hear appeals against the Metropolitan, and could summon him before his court to judge the validity or legality of his acts; he could

H 2

thus exercise a continuous supervision over the Russian Church. East Roman architects designed, and East Roman artists adorned the new sanctuaries. The earliest Russian law-book which we possess—the *Russkaya Pravda*—was compiled, it would seem, by ecclesiastics for the ecclesiastical courts; in form it is modelled on the Byzantine manuals—the Ecloga and the Prochiron—and when in course of time custom even in the civil courts gave place to written law, this ecclesiastical code formed a precedent which was followed by the State in its own legislation.

The result of this intimate connection with the Eastern Church was that from the first Russia felt out of sympathy with the Roman Catholic nations of the West, and was thus drawn into ever closer relations with the Eastern Slavs and the Roman Empire. Although dogma remained unchanged, ecclesiastical practice was altered by the recognition of national custom and usage, and this national sentiment within the church was only confirmed by the fact that just as in the history of the Empire, so in Russia it was ultimately found that Metropolitan and monarch needed each other's mutual support; there was no feud between Church and State, as in the West, while in the crusade against the Mongols both State and Church were strengthened by their common action against the Asiatic invader. The prince receiving his office with religious ceremonies is the protector of the orthodox church—though not of heretics

—is the servant of God, and is under the duty of listening to the moral counsel of his priests, while the latter, as being the only learned folk in the realm, were the teachers of the nation, and for the same reason were constantly employed in matters of state.

In the same way Russia absorbed the monastic piety of East Rome : for the great Pechersky monastery of Kiev its abbot Theodosius adopted the rule of Theodore the Studite, while, again following Byzantine practice, the monasteries were used as prisons for deposed and conquered princes. At the time when Russia received Christianity the orthodox faith had been once for all determined, so that there are no great dogmatic struggles in the early history of the Russian Church; but the Russian monarch occupied towards his clergy the same position as the Emperor and claimed a right to intervene in the government of the Church. The Tsar summoned synods, deposed bishops, and even decided disputes in matters of discipline, as in the burning question as to whether it is the duty of a Christian to fast on Wednesdays and Fridays, if a Church festival should happen to fall on one of those days.

After the capture of Constantinople by the Turks the Russian Church became in large measure the heir of the Church of the Empire : it was granted its independence by the Eastern patriarchates, and the Russian hierarchy was given the right to elect their own Metropolitan; the latter was made superior to all othe᷄

Metropolitans, and ranked next after the Patriarchs : he himself was recognised as a Patriarch at the end of the sixteenth century.

The Russian sovereign may in the same way be regarded as the heir of the Byzantine emperors. A Russian scholar has recently shown that the coronation ceremony of the princes of Moscow reproduced the forms of the coronation of the Byzantine " Cæsar," *i.e.* the chosen successor of the reigning emperor. When Peter the Great abolished the Russian Patriarchate and put in its place the Holy Synod (1723), this was only possible because of the view of the relations of Church and State which Russia had inherited from East Rome : a Western emperor might support a rival Pope, he would never have dreamed of abolishing the Papacy. To the West a Church without a Pope was unthinkable.

Thus for the whole Slav world to-day Byzantine history is modern history : for Serbia and Bulgaria at their greatest owed most to East Rome, and the history of Russia can only be understood aright through a knowledge of that Empire from which she has inherited so mighty a tradition.

EPILOGUE

ONE question remains : What was the essential character of this Byzantine civilisation? That question is hotly disputed. The conviction has often been expressed that the Empire of East Rome was " a strictly Oriental empire." In the course of the present sketch it has been freely admitted that the civilisation of East Rome had absorbed many Oriental elements, alike in art, in criminal law, and even in its theory of sovereignty. But, in the view of the present writer, it is not the Orient which gave to Byzantine civilisation its essential character : that character is rather derived from a fusion of two traditions —the Hellenistic tradition of the Greek cities of the eastern Mediterranean, and the Roman tradition which New Rome received from the early Empire. In the Byzantine Empire the fusion of those two traditions is so complete that the elements belonging to each are only with difficulty to be isolated. But it may be said broadly that in language, in literature, in theology and cult East Rome is Greek and is intensely conscious of that fact : in its law and its military tradition, in its diplomacy, its fiscal policy and its consistent maintenance of the supremacy of the state it is Roman. This is no place for a detailed discussion of the problem : here only a dogmatic statement is possible; the separate chapters of this little book will have declared the view of its author. That view is briefly this : that for any vital understanding of the Byzantine Empire it is essential to realise that the civilisation of that empire was *continuous with* a past that was both Greek and Roman. Whatever elements the West of Europe inherited from the Empire —and Dopsch has recently suggested that these were more numerous and more important than historians have often recognised—these elements were yet inadequate to represent a continuity in civilisation. There is a break in the development of Western Europe which has no parallel in the Eastern Empire. The continuity within the Byzantine Empire of the Hellenistic tradition in thought and language and literature needs no reinforcement here; but the importance in that empire of the preservation of the Roman conception of state supremacy may be briefly illustrated. We can thus gather up and link together some aspects of the life of East Rome with which we have already become familiarised.

It is indeed this survival of the Roman conception of the supremacy of the state and of the central government which not only gives its unity to Byzantine history, but in large measure determines the whole development of the civilisation of East Rome. Herein lies its fundamental distinction from the development of Western Europe. In the East there is *one* state in which all authority is highly centralised; in Western Europe of the Middle Ages there is a welter of small states : " the world of the small state *is* the Middle Ages " —Kleinstaaterei *ist* Mittelalter. And within these small states authority and jurisdiction are alike decentralised: innumerable local courts and local administrative bodies strain every nerve in an endeavour to keep at arm's length the royal power and the emissaries of the king. In the West the Austinian jurist must pile legal fiction upon legal fiction—a veritable Pelion upon Ossa—before he can reconstruct any such sovereignty as his orderly soul craves. East Rome is the Austinian's Paradise; for in that remote and hieratic symbol of sovereignty, the Byzantine Emperor, was vested in its entirety the supreme *imperium* which is the spinal cord of Roman constitutional history, the conception which links early Roman king to Republican consul, Republican consul to the principate of Augustus, and that principate to the God-sustained monarchy of a Byzantine autocrat.

Constantine, we have seen, was at once the first Christian Emperor and the ruler who reasserted the supremacy of the Roman State. That supremacy became an axiom of the political life of New Rome: that supremacy the Church of the Byzantine Empire was powerless to destroy. The Church accepted the consequences of that fact, and secured its own position by the practical proof that the civil state could not forgo ecclesiastical support. But by that acceptance it necessarily fettered its own independent action, for in the last resort the sovereign could always depose a refractory Patriarch. Cerularius failed in his attempt to create an East Roman Papacy: the Patriarch remained "the minister for

Religion." In the West the sovereignty of the centralised state did not outlive the barbarian invasions; and because there was no such tradition of state supremacy as a vital force, the Church could claim and assert her own freedom. Innocent III and Gregory VII have no parallels in East Rome.

When once in Western Europe the fiscal system of the Empire had broken down, no barbarian king could restore the complex machinery which the Roman administration had maintained. The West lapsed of necessity into a landed economy. But East Rome preserved its money economy; and as part and parcel of that money economy the East Roman State tenaciously asserted its right to tax its subjects according to its own good pleasure. It refused to accept in exchange for that right the straitly covenanted services of Western feudalism : no Byzantine subject raised the plea that his sovereign must " live of his own." On the revenue derived from this taxation were based the standing army, the diplomacy and the administration of the East Roman Cæsars; these essential supports of the throne the emperor did not sustain of his subjects' grace : they were his rightful appanage.

And part of this heritage of state supremacy was the Empire's single system of law—that law which emanated from the fount of all authority, the Emperor, and which had behind it the sanction and the prestige of the centuries. Just as the Church was powerless to under-

mine the authority of the State, so it was
unable to effect—rather, it would seem never
to have seriously contemplated—a remodel-
ling of the State's law. It never attempted by
the practical application of Christian principles
radically to revise a legal code which was
rooted and grounded in the frank acceptance
of a pagan egoism. What Mohammedanism
successfully achieved, the Christian Church left
to heretic Iconoclast sovereigns, then roundly
cursed their work and returned resolutely to
the Roman tradition. But in the West the
single law perished with the single state whose
creation it was. The law of medieval England
is local law, customary law, folk law; and the
idea of a sole legislative authority must fight
hard for recognition. And since there is no
one civil law inherited from a pagan state, a
Christian law can arise; guilt is not necessarily determined by human evidence : for
such fallible proof is substituted the judgment
of Heaven, and trial by ordeal can take the
place of the witness of man.

The triumph of the State is also the triumph
of centralisation : power is concentrated
within the walls of Constantinople. A nobility
may own vast domains in the provinces, but
wealth is *used* within the capital. The Eastern
Empire, by maintaining its tradition of a
centralised state, never develops a local feudal
nobility on the Western pattern. The feudal
nobility of the Byzantine Empire is irresistibly drawn to the centre of the Empire's
life : it employs the revenues derived from its

provincial estates to purchase preferment at
Court, and its constant aim is thus to enter
into the narrow circle of a nobility of office
which finds its natural home in Constantinople.
In general, therefore, the feudal nobility of
East Rome does not oppose the sovereign as
a united class, for the aim of each powerful
noble is to seize to himself the supreme position
of power—to be hailed as Emperor in Constantine's city. Since this is the great magnet,
nobles may be for a time confederates, but
they are at heart rivals, and an emperor can
often defeat one rebel by turning against
him another provincial baron. The Seljuk
gained Asia Minor because the great military
captains had their eyes set on one goal—
Constantinople: for he who was lord of
Constantinople was master of the destinies of
men, since he was master of the administration, and master also of the wealth which
flowed from all the provinces to the centre
of the Empire.

This tradition of state supremacy and the
bureaucracy which maintained it moulded the
forms of the Empire's life. East Rome, like
the Rome of the West, was extraordinarily
catholic in its welcome to the stranger: if he
would accept the Empire's religious belief,
Persian or Armenian, Slav or Bulgar, Russian
or Briton, each could find a place in her
service. The Empire drew its talent from
many sources. But these foreigners and
adventurers came as individuals, and they were
merged in a system. They brought, doubt-

less, new vigour to the system, but the system itself was incredibly old; it was stronger than they. They did not—they could not—remodel the system. The framework of Byzantine life remains essentially the same, and every revival of the East Roman State takes the form of a reassertion of tradition. It is this which gives to the superficial observer of the Empire's history an impression of unchanging rigidity. That impression vanishes on closer study; but it *is* true that, though no century of Byzantine history is like any other century, life does tend to express itself through inherited moulds. Before the conquest of Constantinople by the Crusaders in A.D. 1204 there is no radical refashioning of the East Roman world. No conqueror introduces into the Empire, as did the Norman into medieval England, another culture and other ways of government. It was only under the sway of the Latins that upon the ruins of the single state which had to the last maintained its inheritance from the ancient world there were founded many feudal principalities. That was the inevitable consequence of the victory of Western Europe. We have returned to our starting-point: for any vital understanding of East Rome it is essential to realise that its civilisation is continuous with its Greek and Roman past.

. . . . . .

The Hellenistic tradition—the Roman tradition: and the fusion of both traditions *is* the Byzantine Empire.

BIBLIOGRAPHY [1]

[See generally K. Krumbacher: *Geschichte der byzantinischen Litteratur* (2nd ed.), Leipzig, 1897, and bibliographies in *Cambridge Medieval History* and *Byzantinische Zeitschrift*. Where no place of publication is stated in this bibliography the book was published in London.]

CHAPTER I. *The City of Constantine.*—For Constantine's religious position every student should read J. Maurice: *Numismatique constantinienne*, Paris, 1908, etc., Vol. II, Introduction, chs. ii and iii, and for a criticism of Maurice *cf.* Bréhier: *Revue historique*, July 1915. Von Schultze goes too far, I think, in his contention that Constantine could have made no concessions to paganism: see his *Altchristliche Städte und Landschaften*, I: *Konstantinopel*, Part I, § 2, Leipzig, 1913. [Contrast T. Preger: *Hermes*, XXXVI (1901), pp. 457–69.] See further, Eduard Schwartz, *Kaiser Constantin und die christliche Kirche*, 2nd ed., Leipzig, 1936; N. H. Baynes, *Constantine the Great and the Christian Church*, 1930, and *Cambridge Ancient History*, Vol. XII (Cambridge, 1939), pp. 678–99, 796–99; and consult the collection of essays edited by F. J. Dölger: *Konstantin der Grosse und seine Zeit*, Freiburg, 1913. For Constantinople *cf.* A. van Millingen: *Constantinople*, 1906; *Byzantine Constantinople* (the walls of the city), 1899; *Byzantine Churches in Constantinople*, 1912; J. Ebersolt, A. Thiers, *Les Eglises de Constantinople*, 2 vols., Paris, 1913 (in the collection *Monuments de l'Art byzantin*). See also W. H. Hutton: *Constantinople*, 1909. *Cf.* G. W. Holmes: *The Age of Justinian and Theodora*, I, ch. i, 1905, and Leclercq's excellent bibliography, s.v. "Byzance" in Cabrol's *Dictionnaire d'Archéologie chrétienne et de Liturgie*, Paris, 1907, etc.

CHAPTER II. *Social Life.*—S. Runciman, *Byzantine Civilisation*, 1923; G. Manojlović, *Le Peuple de Constantinople* (written in 1904), Byzantion, XI (1936), pp. 617–716; A. H. M. Jones, *The Greek City from Alexander to Justinian*,

[1] Revised for Fourth Impression, 1943.

Oxford, 1940; J. G. Winter, *Life and Letters in the Papyri*, University of Michigan Press, 1933; J. W. Holmes: *The Age of Justinian and Theodora*, I, pp. 83–126, 1905; C. Diehl: *Figures byzantines*, 2 vols., Paris, 1906, 1908; his *Dans l'Orient byzantin*, Paris, 1917, his *Choses et Gens de Byzance*, Paris, 1926, his *La Société byzantine à l'époque des Comnènes*, Paris, 1929, and his *Théodora*, Paris, n.d.; K. Dieterich: *Byzantinische Charakterköpfe*, Leipzig, 1909, and his *Hofleben in Byzanz.* (Voigtlander's *Quellenbücher*, 19); J. Ebersolt: *Mélanges d'Histoire et d'Archéologie Byz.*, Paris, 1917; H. Gelzer: *Ausgewählte kleine Schriften*, Leipzig, 1907; A. Rambaud: *Études sur l'histoire byzantine*, Paris, 1912; Milton Vance: *Beiträge zur byz. Kulturgeschichte*, Jena, 1907; M. Hamilton: *Incubation*, St. Andrews, 1906; Karl Roth: *Sozial und Kulturgeschichte des Byzantinischen Reiches* (*Sammlung Göschen*), Berlin and Leipzig, 1919; N. Turchi: *La Civiltà bizantina*, Turin, 1915; and A. Heisenberg: in *Staat und Gesellschaft der Griechen und Römer bis zum Ausgang des Mittelalters*, 2nd ed., Leipzig, 1923. See further, G. Buckler, *Anna Comnena*, 1929, and G. La Piana, *The byzantine Theater*, Speculum, XI (1936), pp. 171–211. Much material will be found in Finlay's *History of Greece*, and above all in the works of Sir W. M. Ramsay. For Byzantine Egypt see H. I. Bell in *Journal of Egyptian Archæology*, IV (1917), pp. 86–106.

CHAPTER III. *The Emperors.*—This little book is not a history of the Empire, and it is impossible to give a long list of large histories or monographs on special periods in this place. It must suffice to say that Gibbon's *Decline and Fall of the Roman Empire* should be read in the edition of J. B. Bury, 7 vols., 1896–1900; new edition 1909–13. Of recent books mention may be made of A. Vasiliev, *Histoire de l'Empire Byzantin*, 2 vols., Paris, 1932; Ernst Stein, *Geschichte des spätrömischen Reiches*, Vol. I, *Vom römischen zum byzantinischen Staate, 284–476 n. Chr.*, Vienna, 1928; H. St. L. B. Moss, *The Birth of the Middle Ages, 395–814*, Oxford, 1935; Ch. Diehl and G. Marçais, *Le Monde oriental de 395 à 1081* (=Histoire du Moyen Age), t. 3 (in the Histoire générale, ed. G. Glotz), Paris, 1936; Luigi Salvatorelli, *L'Italia medioevale dalle invasioni barbariche agli inizi del secolo xi* (=Storia d'Italia, vol. 3), Milano, n.d.; A. A. Vasiliev, *Byzance et les Arabes*, Tome I, 820–67, Brussels, 1935; H. Pirenne, *Mohammed and*

Charlemagne, 1939; L. Halphen, *Les Barbarês : des grandes invasions aux conquêtes turques du XIe Siècle*, 3rd ed., Paris, 1936; R. Grousset, *Histoire des Croisades et du Royaume franc de Jérusalem*, 3 vols., Paris, 1934–36. There are good outlines of Byzantine history by von Scala in Helmolt's *History of the World*, Vol. V (English translation); by N. Jorga: *The Byzantine Empire* (Temple Primers); and by Charles Diehl: *Histoire de l'Empire byzantin*, Paris, 1919 (English translation, published by the Princeton University Press, 1925), and *cf.* his *Byzance, Grandeur et Décadence*, Paris, 1919: more popular sketches by C. W. C. Oman: 1892, and E. A. Foord: 1911. See also Gerland in *The Catholic Encyclopœdia* and J. B. Bury (s.v. "Roman Empire, Later") in *Encyclopœdia Britannica* (11th ed.); also H. Gelzer in Krumbacher's *Gesch. d. byz. Litteratur* (2nd ed.), Leipzig, 1897; and *cf.* F. Harrison: *Among my Books*, ch. x, 1912. For reference, *Cambridge Medieval History*, Vol. IV, 1923.

CHAPTER IV. *Byzantine Sovereignty.*—There is a considerable scattered literature, and *cf.* especially A. Gasquet: *De l'Autorité impériale en matière religieuse à Byzance*, Paris, 1879; and his *L'Empire byzantin et la Monarchie franque*, Paris, 1888; further, K. M. Setton, *Christian Attitude towards the Emperor in the Fourth Century*, New York, 1941; A. Grabar, *L'empereur dans l'art byzantin*, Paris, 1936; A. Alföldi, *Die Ausgestaltung des monarchischen Zeremoniells am römischen Kaiserhofe*, Mitt. Deutsch. Arch. Inst., Röm. Abt. 49 (1934), pp. 1–118 (Munich); Ch. Diehl, *Le palais impérial et la vie de cour à Byzance*, Revue de Paris, 1st Jan. 1935, pp. 82–98. J. B. Bury: *The Constitution of the Later Roman Empire*, Cambridge, 1910 (with references to literature in notes); A. Rambaud: *Études sur l'histoire byz.*, ch. iv, Paris, 1912; L. Hahn in *Das Erbe der Alten*, Heft vi, Leipzig, 1913; and for the earlier development O. Hirschfeld: *Die Kaiserlichen Verwaltungsbeamten bis auf Diocletian* (2nd ed.), esp. pp. 466–86, Berlin, 1905. For Eusebius and the Christian theory of Empire: *Annuaire de l'Institut de Philol. et d'Hist. Orientales*, II (Brussels), pp. 13–18; for Byzantine diplomatic usage see K. Brandi in *Archiv für Urkundenforschung*, I (1908), pp. 5–86; R. Helm, *ibid.*, XII (1931–2), pp. 375–436; F. Dölger, *Historische Zeitschrift*, CLIX (1938–39), pp. 299–50; G. Ostrogorsky, *Seminarium Kondokovianum*, VIII (1936), pp. 41–61.

CHAPTER V. *The Church.*—Very much remains to be done before a satisfactory history of the Greek Church can be written. For a general outline *cf.* A. Fortescue: *The Orthodox Eastern Church* (3rd ed.), 1911 (R. C.); W. F. Adeney: *The Greek and Eastern Churches*, Edinburgh, 1908 (Protestant); H. F. Tozer: *The Church and the Eastern Empire*, 1897. Best studies known to me on characteristics of Greek Church; Sir W. M. Ramsay: *Luke the Physician*, ch. iv, 1908; Prinz Max Herzog von Sachsen: *Vorlesungen über die orientalische Kirchenfrage*, Freiburg, 1907; *cf.* H. Gelzer: *Vom heiligen Berge*, etc., Leipzig, 1904, and his *Geistliches u. Weltliches aus dem türkisch-griechischen Orient*, Leipzig, 1900. For special periods *cf.* for fourth century P. Batiffol: *La Paix Constantinienne*, etc., Paris, 1914; L. Duchesne: *The Early History of the Church*, Vols. II and III, 1912 and 1924, and his *L'Église au VIᵉ Siècle*, Paris, 1925; for the rivalry between the Patriarchs of Alexandria and Constantinople: *Journal of Egyptian Archæology*, XII (1926), pp. 145–56; K. Lübeck: *Reichseinteilung und kirchliche Hierarchie des Orients*, Münster, 1901; for Greek Monasticism see Holl: *Preussische Jahrbücher*, XCIV (1898), pp. 407–24; F. W. Hasluck: *Athos and its Monasteries*, 1924; R. M. Dawkins: *The Monks of Athos*, 1936; W. K. Lowther Clarke has translated *The Ascetic Works of Saint Basil*, 1925; for sixth-century missions, L. Duchesne: *Églises Séparées* (2nd ed.), Paris, 1905; and for Christianity in the East, J. Labourt: *Le Christianisme dans l'Empire perse* (2nd ed.), Paris, 1904; for the Monophysite controversy, W. A. Wigram: *The Separation of the Monophysites*, 1923; for history A.D. 527–847, J. Pargoire: *L'Église byzantine*, Paris, 1905; for Iconoclasm, L. Bréhier: *La Querelle des Images* (2nd ed., with bibliography), Paris, 1902; E. J. Martin: *A History of the Iconoclastic Controversy* (1930); G. Ostrogorsky, *Les débuts de la querelle des Images*, Mélanges Diehl (Paris, 1930), I, pp. 235–55; and his *Studien zur Geschichte des byzantinischen Bilderstreites*, Breslau, 1929; and see the article "Images" in the *Dictionnaire d'Archéologie chrétienne et de Liturgie*, Paris; for the Papacy: Erich Caspar: *Geschichte des Papsttums*, 2 vols., Tübingen, 1930, 1933 (an unfinished work); W. Norden, *Das Papsttum und Byzanz*, Berlin, 1903; for the breach with Rome, the best general sketch is F. X. Seppelt's "Das Papsttum und Byzanz," in M. Sdralek's

Kirchengeschichtliche Abhandlungen, Vol. II, Breslau, 1904;
and *cf.* J. Ruinaut: *Le Schisme de Photius*, Paris, 1910,
and L. Bréhier: *Le Schisme Oriental du XIᵉ Siècle*, Paris,
1899 (both with bibliographies); for relations between
Church and State, H. Gelzer: *Ausgewählte kleine Schriften*,
ch. ii, Leipzig, 1907; V. Şesan: *Kirche und Staat*, Vol. I,
Czernowitz, 1911; and J. B. Bury: *The Constitution of the
Later Roman Empire*, Cambridge, 1910. For the later
period see Bréhier: *L'Église et l'Orient au Moyen Age*
(2nd ed.), Paris, 1907; and J. M. Hussey: *Church and
Learning in the Byzantine Empire, 867–1185*, 1937. For
Paganism, G. Boissier: *La Fin du Paganisme* (4th ed.),
Paris, 1903; and P. de Labriolle, *La Réaction païenne*,
Paris, 1934; for Islam, C. H. Becker: *Christentum u.
Islam*, Tübingen, 1907; and *Islamstudien*, Leipzig, 1924;
and for the Stylite Saints, Delehaye: *Les Saints Stylites*,
Brussels, 1923, and H. Lietzmann: *Das Leben des heiligen
Symeon Stylites*, Leipzig, 1908. For Byzantine church
music, H. J. W. Tillyard: *Byzantine Music and Hymno-
graphy*, 1923; E. Wellesz: *Byzantinische Musik*, Breslau,
1927, and his *Trésor de musique byzantine*, Paris, 1935;
see *Byzantion*, XI (1936), pp. 729–37.

CHAPTER VI. *Landholding*, etc.—All the literature on
this subject is highly technical, and much of the best
work is in the Russian language; but *cf.* O. Seeck:
Geschichte des Untergangs der antiken Welt, Vol. II,
Book III, ch. vi; for landholding and agrarian conditions
in the Byzantine Empire, G. Ostrogorsky: *Cambridge
Economic History* (Cambridge, 1941), Vol. I, pp. 194–223,
full bibliography pp. 579–83; G. Stadtmüller in *Neue
Jahrbücher für deutsche Wissenschaft*, XIII (1937), pp. 421–
38; F. Dölger in *Bulletin of the International Committee of
Historical Sciences* (Washington), V (1933), pp. 5–15, and
see E. R. Hardy, Junr.: *The Large Estates of Byzantine
Egypt*, New York, 1931; G. J. Bratianu: *Études byzantines
d'histoire économique et sociale*, Paris, 1938. For taxation,
G. Ostrogorsky: *Vierteljahrschrift für Sozial- und Wirt-
schaftsgeschichte*, XX (1927), pp. 1–108, *ibid.*, XXII (1929),
pp. 129–43; *Byzantion*, VI (1931), pp. 229–40; G.
Rouillard: *Mélanges Diehl* (Paris, 1930), I, pp. 277–89.
On the influence of the patronus, the best general study
is perhaps H. Monnier's *Méditation sur la Constitution
Εκατερωι et le Jus Pœnitendi*, Paris, 1900; but see also
F. de Zulueta: "De Patrociniis Vicorum" in Vol. I of

Vinogradoff's *Oxford Studies in Social and Legal History*.
For a later period *cf.* Rambaud: *L'Empire grec*, Paris,
1870; G. Testaud: *Des Rapports des Puissants et des petits
Propriétaires ruraux*, etc., Bordeaux, 1898, and C.
Neumann: *Die Weltstellung des byz. Reiches*, Leipzig, 1894.
For the colonatus see bibliography in M. Rostowzew:
Studien zur Geschichte d. röm. Kolonats, Leipzig, 1910, and
Roth Clausing: *The Roman Colonate*, New York, 1925.
For the Farmer's Law, the fullest discussion is by
Panchenko in *Izvyestiya IX* of the Russian Archæological
Institute in Constantinople, but see W. Ashburner in
Journal of Hellenic Studies, 1910, 1912, and *cf. Rivista
storico-critica delle Scienze teologiche*, February and April
1906. Further, consult the studies of Monnier in *Nouvelle
Revue historique*, etc., Vols. XVI, XVIII and XIX on the
Epibolé, and for Protimesis, M. G. Platon's work on
that subject, Paris, 1906, and generally his *La Démocratie
et le Régime fiscal*, Paris, 1899, and H. Gelzer: *Byz.
Kulturgeschichte*, ch. v, Tübingen, 1909.

CHAPTER VII. *The Civil Administration.*—The only
full treatment for the earlier period is in O. Karlowa:
Römische Rechtsgeschichte, I, Leipzig, 1885; but there is a
brief sketch in T. Mommsen: *Abriss des röm. Staatsrechts*
(2nd ed.), Leipzig, 1907; and see O. Seeck: *Geschichte des
Untergangs der antiken Welt* (2nd ed., 1897, etc.), Vols. I
and II, and *Cambridge Medieval History*, Vol. I, ch. ii,
1911, with Bury: *History of the Later Roman Empire*,
Vol. I, ch. ii, London, 1923. For the reign of Justinian
cf. Diehl: *Justinien*, pp. 269–313, Paris, 1901. For provincial administration, G. Rouillard: *L'Administration
civile de l'Égypte byzantine*, 2nd ed., Paris, 1928; Diehl:
*Études sur l'administration byzantine dans l'Exarchat de
Ravenne*, Paris, 1888 (with bibliography); M. Gelzer:
Studien zur byzantinischen Verwaltung Ägyptens, Leipzig,
1909; and U. Wilcken: *Grundzüge u. Chrestomathie der
Papyruskunde*, Vol. I, *Hist. Teil.*, Leipzig, 1912. For the
later period the one essential work is Bury: *The Imperial
Administrative System in the Ninth Century*, 1911 (with
bibliography). See further, E. Kuhn: *Die städtische und
bürgerliche Verfassung des röm. Reiches*, Leipzig, 1865; and
for the administration of justice, Zachariae von Lingenthal:
Geschichte d. griechisch-röm. Rechts (3rd ed.), Berlin, 1892.
For finance, O. Seeck: *Geschichte des Untergangs*, etc.,
Vol. II, Book III, ch. vi; Bury: *A History of the Eastern*

Roman Empire, ch. vii, 1912; Andréadès in *Finanz-Archiv*, Year XXVI, Vol. II, pp. 1–28; F. Dölger: *Beiträge zur Geschichte der byzantinischen Finanzverwaltung*, Byzantinisches Archiv, IX (1927); A. Andréadès: *Byzantinische Zeitschrift*, XXVIII (1928), pp. 287–323; and L. M. Hartmann: *Ein Kapitel vom spätantiken u. frühmittelalterlichen Staate*, Berlin, 1913; and *cf.* A. Andréadès: *Le Montant du Budget de l'Empire byzantin*, Paris, 1922.

CHAPTER VIII.—*The Army and Navy.*

Army.—For the Roman army down to the seventh century see R. Grosse: *Römische Militärgeschichte von Gallienus bis zum Beginn der byzantinischen Themenverfassung*, Berlin, 1920 (with bibliography). There is no general history of the later Roman army: a good sketch will be found in C. Oman: *A History of the Art of War: The Middle Ages*, Book IV, 1898. There are numerous articles, most of them written by Russian scholars, which cannot be detailed here, but the student will be able to trace the historical development in the following:—Prior to Justinian, T. Mommsen: *Hermes*, XXIX, Heft 2, Berlin, 1889 (*Gesammelte Schriften*, Vol. VI); R. Cagnat: *L'Armée romaine d'Afrique* (2nd ed.), Paris, 1912. Justinian's reign, C. Diehl: *Justinien*, pp. 145–246 (and bibliography), and his *L'Afrique byzantine*, Paris, 1896; *cf.* J. Maspero: *L'Organisation Militaire de l'Égypte byzantine*, Paris, 1912; and V. Chapot: *La Frontière de l'Euphrate*, Paris, 1907. For later sixth century, F. Aussaresses: *L'Armée byzantine*, Paris, 1909. System of Themes, H. Gelzer: *Die Genesis der byz. Themenverfassung*, Leipzig, 1899; C. Diehl: *Études byzantines*, pp. 276–92, Paris, 1905. Ninth century, J. B. Bury: *A History of the Eastern Roman Empire*, pp. 221–29, and his *Imperial Administrative System*, etc., pp. 39–68, pp. 106 sqq. and bibliography. Tenth century, A. Rambaud: *L'Empire grec*, Part III, Paris, 1870; R. Gaignerot: *Des Bénéfices militaires*, etc., Bordeaux, 1898; and much information in Schlumberger's various works. Eleventh century, C. Neumann: *Die Weltstellung des byz. Reiches*, Leipzig, 1894 (and in French translation). Twelfth century, F. Chalandon: *Jean II Comnène*, etc., pp. 609–22, Paris, 1912. For Byzantine poliorcetics see *Abhandlungen d. kön. Gesellschaft d. Wissenschaften zu Göttingen*, N.F., Vol. XI, No. 1, Berlin, 1908.

Navy.—A. F. Gfrörer: *Byzantinische Geschichten*, Vol. II,

ch. xxii, Graz, 1874; K. Neumann: " Die byzantinische
Marine," *Historische Zeitschrift*, Vol. XLV (1898), pp. 1
sqq.; H. Gelzer: *Die Genesis der byz. Themenverfassung*
(as above), pp. 30 sqq.; Diehl: *Études byz.* (as above),
pp. 280 sqq.; J. B. Bury: *The Imperial Administrative
System*, etc., pp. 108 sqq., and his " The Naval Policy of
the Roman Empire in Relation to the Western Provinces,"
Centenario della Nascita di Michele Amari, Vol. II, pp.
21–34, Palermo, 1910.

CHAPTER IX. *Education.*—My chapter is compiled on
the basis of the materials collected by F. Schemmel in
numerous studies (in the *Neue Jahrbücher für das klassische
Altertum*, etc.) published during recent years, and in his
Die Hochschule von Konstantinopel vom V bis IX Jhdt.,
Berlin, 1912. J. Walden: *The Universities of Ancient
Greece*, London, 1913 (with good bibliography). For the
later period see F. Fuchs: *Die höheren Schulen von
Konstantinopel im Mittelalter*, Leipzig, 1926; J. M. Hussey:
Church and Learning, etc. (*supra*); J. B. Bury: *A History
of the Eastern Roman Empire*, pp. 434–49; and *cf.* Bréhier,
in *Byzantion*, IV (1927), pp. 13–28.

CHAPTER X. *Literature.*—The great encyclopædia on
the subject is K. Krumbacher: *Geschichte der byz. Litteratur*
(2nd ed.), Leipzig, 1897, and see his article "Greek Literature: Byzantine" in *Encyclopædia Britannica* (11th ed.),
and *cf. Die griechische u. lateinische Litteratur* (2nd ed.),
Leipzig, 1907 (in *Die Kultur der Gegenwart*). For a
different view *cf.* K. Dieterich: *Geschichte der byzantinischen
u. neugriechischen Litteratur*, Leipzig, 1902; his *Byzantinische Charakterköpfe*, Leipzig, 1909, and his article
"Byzantine Literature" (with bibliography) in *The
Catholic Encyclopædia*, Vol. III. For references to recent
work see Gerhard Rauschen: *Patrologie*, ed. B. Altaner,
Freiburg, 1931. See also G. Montelatici: *Storia della
Litteratura bizantina*, Milan, 1916. Further, *cf.* T. R.
Glover: *Life and Letters in the Fourth Century*, Cambridge,
1901; von Christ: *Geschichte der griechischen Litteratur*,
Teil II, Hälfte II (5th ed.), Munich, 1913; von Fleschen-
berg: *Entwicklungsgeschichte des griechischen Romanes im
Altertum*, § 14, Halle, 1913; C. Neumann: *Griechische
Geschichtsschreiber und Geschichtsquellen*, Leipzig, 1888;
D. C. Hesseling: *Essai sur la Civilisation byzantine* (French
translation), Paris, 1907; and for the influence of the
West in the later period, J. B. Bury: *Romances of Chivalry*

on Greek Soil, Oxford, 1911. For a monograph on a Byzantine poet *cf.* A. Veniero: *Paolo Silenziario*, Catania, 1916. Mrs Buckler's monograph on *Anna Comnena* appeared in 1929. For the influence of East Roman thought on Western Europe *cf.* J. de Ghellinck: *Le Mouvement théologique du XIIe Siècle*, Paris, 1914. In the Loeb Classical Library there are English translations of the history of Ammianus Marcellinus, of the letters of St. Basil, of the works of Procopius and of the Greek Anthology. A. FitzGerald has produced an English translation of *The Letters of Synesius of Cyrene*, 1926, and of his *Essays and Hymns*, 1930. Dr E. A. S. Dawes has translated *The Alexiad of the Princess Anna Comnena*, 1928, and E. Renauld has published a French translation of Psellos' history of his own time, 2 vols., Paris, 1926, 1928.

CHAPTER XI. *Art.*—C. Diehl: *Manuel d'Art byzantin*, 2nd ed., 2 vols., Paris, 1925, 1926, and O. M. Dalton: *Byzantine Art and Archæology*, have both good bibliographies, as has Leclercq's article "Byzantin" (Art) in *Dictionnaire d'Archéologie chrétienne et de Liturgie*, Paris, 1907, etc. Further, C. Bayet: *L'Art byzantin* (3rd ed.), Paris, 1904 (?); Diehl: *Études byzantines*, pp. 153–81, Paris, 1905; Millet: "L'Art byzantin," in Michel: *Histoire de l'Art*, I, Paris, 1905; L. Bréhier: *Les Églises byzantines* (2nd ed.), Paris, n.d.; and his *Les Origines du Crucifix* (3rd ed.), Paris, 1908, and in *Byzantinische Zeitschrift*, XII (1903), pp. 153–81; W. R. Lethaby: *Medieval Art*, 1904; J. Strzygowski: *Origin of Christian Church Art*, Oxford, 1923, with bibliography of his earlier works; O. M. Dalton: *East Christian Art*, Oxford, 1925; D. T. Rice, *Byzantine Art*, Oxford, 1935; G. Duthuit: *Byzance et l'art du XIIe Siècle*, Paris, 1926 (in the series *La culture moderne*); E. Diez and O. Demus: *Byzantine Mosaics in Greece*, Harvard University Press, 1931; for the work of the American Byzantine Institute see the three Preliminary Reports of T. Whittemore, 1933–1942: *The Mosaics of Haghia Sophia at Istanbul*, Boston; J. Ebersolt: *La Miniature byzantine*, Paris and Brussels, 1926 (reproduction of 140 miniatures); Charles Diehl (in Histoire de l'Art byzantin): *La Peinture byzantine*, Paris, 1933 (96 plates); Louis Bréhier: *La Sculpture et les Arts mineurs byzantins* (in Histoire de l'Art byzantin), Paris, 1936 (96 plates). There is a sumptuously produced French series of volumes on *Monuments de l'Art byzantin* (1899–1927), Paris. There is a general study by O. Wulff: *Altchristliche und byzantin-ische Kunst*, Berlin (1915); and *cf.* J. Ebersolt: *Les Arts somptuaires de Byzance*, Paris, 1923. For illustrations cf. *Great Buildings and how to enjoy them: Byzantine Archi-tecture*, by Edith A. Browne, 1912; and in the series *Die Kunst des Ostens*, Vol. VIII, *Die christliche Kunst des Ostens* by Heinrich Glück, Berlin, 1923; H. Pierce and R. Tyler: *Byzantine Art*, 1926 (100 plates).

CHAPTER XII. *Later Roman Law.*—Zachariae von Lingenthal: *Geschichte des griechisch-röm. Rechts* (3rd ed.), Berlin, 1892; E. H. Freshfield: *Roman Law in the later Roman Empire*, Cambridge, 1932; L. S. Villanueva: *Diritto Bizantino*, Milan, 1906, and A. Albertoni: *Per una Esposizione del diritto bizantino con riguardo all' Italia*, Imola, 1927, both have excellent bibliographies. There is a monograph by H. Monnier on *Les Novelles de Léon le Sage*, Bordeaux, 1923. For the earlier period see H. F. Jolowicz, *Historical Introduction to the Study of Roman Law*, Cam-bridge, 1932 ; R. Sohm's *Institutes of Roman Law* [English translation by Ledlie (3rd ed.), Oxford, 1907]; and opening chapters of H. J. Roby's *Introduction to Justinian's Digest*, Cambridge, 1884; together with H. S. Alivisatos: *Die kirchliche Gesetzgebung des Kaisers Justinian I*, Berlin, 1913; and H. Goudy's article on Roman Law in *Encyclopædia Britannica* (11th ed.). On customary law and its influence on the later development *cf.* L. Mitteis: *Reichsrecht u. Volksrecht in den östlichen Provinzen des röm. Kaiserreichs*, Leipzig, 1891; P. Collinet: *Études historiques sur le Droit de Justinien*, Vol. I, Paris, 1912; and S. Brassloff: *Zur Kenntniss des Volksrechts in den romanisirten Ostprovinzen des röm. Kaiserreiches*, Weimar, 1902.

CHAPTER XIII. *Trade.*—W. G. Holmes: *The Age of Justinian and Theodora*, I, pp. 182–94, 1905; C. Diehl: *Justinien*, pp. 533–45; H. Gelzer: *Byzantinische Kultur-geschichte*, ch. vii, Tübingen, 1909. The two principal works on the subject are W. Heyd (best in French transla-tion): *Histoire du Commerce du Levant au Moyen Age*, Paris, 1885, reprint 1923; and A. Schaube: *Handels-geschichte der romanischen Völker des Mittelmeergebiets*, Munich, etc., 1906. For Syrian traders *cf.* Scheffer-Boichorst in *Mitteilungen des Instituts für österreichische Geschichtsforschung*, VI (1885), pp. 521–50; and L. Bréhier in *Byz. Zeitschrift*, XII (1903), pp. 1–39. For the introduction of the silkworm into the Byzantine Empire:

R. Hennig in *Byzantinische Zeitschrift*, XXXIII (1933), pp. 295–312. For the Book of the Prefect, edition by J. Nicole, Geneva, 1893; and French translation, Geneva, 1904; English translations by A. E. R. Boak: *Journal of Economic and Business History*, I (1928–29), pp. 597–619, and E. H. Freshfield: *Roman Law in the Later Roman Empire: Byzantine Guilds, Professional and Commercial*, Cambridge, 1938; A. Stöckle: *Spätrömische und byzantinische Zünfte*, Klio, Beiheft 9, Leipzig, 1911; and H. Gehrig in Hildebrand's *Jahrbuecher für Nationalökonomie und Statistik*, 3 *Folge*, Vol. XXXVIII (1909), pp. 577–96, together with C. M. Macri: *L'Organisation de l'Économie Urbaine dans Byzance sous la dynastie de Macédoine (867–1057)*, Paris, 1925. *Cf.* P. Boissonade: *Le Travail dans l'Europe chrétienne au Moyen Age*, Paris, 1921, chs. iii–v; and G. Ostrogorsky: "Löhne und Preise in Byzanz," *Byzantinische Zeitschrift*, XXXII (1932), pp. 293–333. For Russian trade, V. O. Kluchevsky: *A History of Russia* (English translation), Vol. I, chs. v and vi, 1911; and A. Vasiliev: "Economic Relations between Byzantium and Old Russia," *Journal of Economic and Business History*, IV (1931–32), pp. 314–34. For Venice, F. C. Hodgson: *The Early History of Venice*, 1901; Kretschmayr: *Geschichte Venedigs*, Vol. I, Gotha, 1905; and R. Heynen: *Zur Entstehung des Kapitalismus in Venedig*, Stuttgart, 1905. For maritime law, W. Ashburner: *The Rhodian Sea-Law*, Oxford, 1909.

CHAPTER XIV. *The Debt of the Slavs.*—For a general historical sketch *cf.* W. Miller: *The Balkans*, 1896; and see his chapters in the *Cambridge Medieval History*, Vol. IV. For the literary dependence, M. Murko: *Geschichte der älteren südslawischen Litteraturen*, Leipzig, 1908; for the mission of Cyril and Methodius *cf.* J. B. Bury: *A History of the Eastern Roman Empire*, ch. xii (and bibliography, pp. 506–7); F. Dvornik: *Les Slaves Byzance et Rome au IXᵉ Siècle*, Paris, 1926; and his book on *Les Légendes de Constantin et de Méthode vues de Byzance*, Prague, 1933. For Bulgaria, C. Jireček: *Geschichte der Bulgaren*, Prague, 1876; Guérin Songeon: *Histoire de la Bulgarie*, Paris, 1913; W. N. S. Slatarski: *Geschichte der Bulgaren*, I (679–1396), Leipzig, 1918 (with useful maps); S. Runciman: *A History of the First Bulgarian Empire*, 1930. For Serbia, H. W. V. Temperley: *History of Serbia*, 1917; C. Jireček: *Geschichte der Serben*,

Vol. I, Gotha, 1911, Vol. II, Part I, 1918; and especially his "Staat und Gesellschaft im mittelalterlichen Serbien" in *Denkschriften* of the Vienna Academy, 1912–1919. For Russia, V. O. Kluchevsky: *A History of Russia* (English translation), 1911, etc.; M. Rostovtzeff: *Iranians and Greeks in South Russia*, Oxford, 1922, ch. ix; L. Goetz: *Staat und Kirche in Altrussland*, Berlin, 1908. For law, F. Sigel: *Lectures on Slavonic Law*, 1902. For Byzantine influence in Rumania, N. Jorga: *La Survivance byzantine dans les pays roumains*, Bukarest, 1913. For Bulgarian Art cf. B. Filow: *L'Ancien Art Bulgare*, Paris, 1922, and his *Early Bulgarian Art*, Berne, 1919. For Serbian Art see G. Millet: *L'ancien Art serbe*, Paris, 1919, and Michael J. Pupin: *South Slav Monuments, I: Serbian Orthodox Church*, London, 1918.

THE EPILOGUE.—*Cf.* the works by Charles Diehl cited in the bibliography to ch. iii for a different view of the character of the Byzantine Empire. See further, James Bryce: *The Holy Roman Empire*, 1915, ch. xvii, which contains some challenging generalisations; A. Heisenberg: "Die Grundlagen der byzantinischen Kultur," *Neue Jahrbuecher für das klassische Altertum*, XXIII (1909), pp. 196–208. The views expressed in this Epilogue have been formed after reading many books which are too numerous to find mention here.

INDEX

Printed by The Riverside Press, Edinburgh